The Deep Water Leaf Society

Harnessing the Transformative Power of Grief

Claire M. Perkins

The Deep Water Leaf Society
Harnessing the Transformative Power of Grief

Copyright 2008, Claire M. Perkins. All Rights Reserved

ISBN 13: 978-0-9821056-1-0
Library of Congress Catalog Number: 2008937129

No part of this book may be reproduced, stored in a mechanical retrieval system, or transmitted in any form by electronic, video, laser, mechanical, photocopying, recoding means or otherwise, in part or in whole, without the written consent of the publisher.
Published by Intuitive Journey Press
Email: claire@intuitivejourney.com

Cover Design and symbols: Kristen Ernst, One Girl's Art, Scottsdale, AZ
http://www.onegirlsart.com

Book Design, Production Coordination: OPA Author Services, Chandler, AZ
http://www.opaauthorservices.com

Copyright and licensing information related to song lyrics reprinted in this work is shown in the Endnotes that follow the text.

Printed on acid-free paper in the United States of America

Table of Contents

Dedication
Acknowledgments i
Preface iv
The Deep Water Leaf Society 1
Cameron's Death 3
Cameron's Life 10
Turtle Soup 20
The Blessing of Padre Pio 27
Saying Goodbye 33
House of Sand 39
Captivity 44
Drowning 52
Every Sparrow that Falls 59
The Music of My Heart 63
Halfway House 66
Voices from the Big Wave 69
Options 85
Black Heart 92
Pollyanna Rising 97
Carved in Stone 104
The Year from Hell 108
The Wish 119
Twins 125
The Medium 133
Turning Point 144

Speak to Me in Music	149
String of Pearls	152
Agreements	156
Tangled Threads	162
The Kidnap of Personal Power	165
Heart Connection	171
Breaking the Bonds of Karma	175
Egypt Calls	181
A Taste of Things to Come	187
The Trip that Was Meant to Be	190
Lizards and Fishes	193
Dreaming Egypt	199
Meeting Menita	201
Desires of the Heart	205
Past and Future Lives	210
Hathor	215
Remembrance	219
The Mythology of Hathor and Sekhmet	225
Do-Overs	228
Epilogue: New Beginnings	234
Author's Note	237
End Notes	

Dedication

*To Cameron, with immense gratitude
and endless love.*

*To Sarah and Ryan, who grew up
in Cameron's shadow
but have always been, and will always be,
equally loved.*

*And, especially, to David,
my love, my strength,
who stood by me through it all,
unselfishly providing me
the time, space and support I needed
to remember who I am.*

Acknowledgments

I am eternally grateful to everyone who contributed to the creation of this book on so many levels. Some played crucial roles in my healing journey and therefore became a part of my story. Others provided hands on support with the physical creation of the book through critique, editing, layout and graphic design. Some offered the moral support and encouragement I needed to see the project through. I offer my deepest appreciation and gratitude to each and every one of you.

To Lucia Capacchione and Marsha Nelson, thank you a thousand times over for bringing the Creative Journal Expressive Arts program to the world. Without the healing tools I learned in the program, my grieving process would have been quite different and I wouldn't have this story to tell. To KC Miller, Linda Bennett and all the teachers at the Southwest Institute of Healing Arts, thank you for creating the Transformational Life Coaching program and infusing it with such spirit and love. To Robert Moss, my deepest thanks for teaching me about the wider reality of dreams and the healing value of imagination and story-telling.

I want to thank Pam Fox and Meredith Davis for following their hearts and dedicating their time and resources to the creation of the Arizona Holistic Chamber of Commerce. It is through that organization that I met many people who were crucial to my healing and to this story. To Jamie Clark, a most gifted psychic medium, thank you so much for validating my sense of continued connection to Cameron. I offer much gratitude to Dorothy Neddermeyer, whose regression work was so helpful to me. To Sherry Anshara, thank you for teaching me how to release old stories and patterns at the cellular level and for giving me a new perspective on karma. To Sheila Reed, I thank you for the gift of Egypt and my introduction to the goddess Sekhmet. It was in Egypt that I finally claimed my voice and discovered the true source of personal power. Without John

The Deep Water Leaf Society

and Carmen LaMarca, the Egypt trip would never have happened—thank you for your role in the synchronicity of it all.

For camaraderie and creative support through the journey of writing, I thank my writers' group: Tiffany Weis, Carolyne Ruck, Barbara Kelly, Mary Keith, Debby Raposa and Dennis Crabtree. Knowing I had you to report to a couple of times each month kept me focused on getting the writing done. I appreciate your insights and constructive criticisms and especially your enthusiasm about the healing value of telling my story.

To Lisa Fraser and Kachina Woman I offer heartfelt thanks for the healing vision you brought me at the outset of my writing project. It was a great gift that carried me through the long months of writing.

I deeply appreciate the thoughtful and thorough editing of Carolyne Ruck, my sister Christine Sinclair and my daughter Sarah Cavender. Your input was invaluable to the accuracy and clarity of the story. I claim full responsibility for any errors that remain, as I may have introduced a few during the course of last minute changes. For handling all the technical aspects of self-publishing, from text layout to final printing, many thanks to Paul McNeese. Without your knowhow, the book would have remained a dream. To Kristen Ernst, a million thanks for creating a cover design that captures so eloquently the theme and feeling of my story.

Without my friends and family to support me along the way, I would not have come through my grief as easily and I would never have written this story. All my thanks and love to each of my dear friends: Dorine, upon whose shoulder I cried through so many Friday lunches; Barbara, who mentored me through a very difficult year with love, support and prayer treatments; Trish, who suffered her own deep losses during the same timeframe, and whose deep and lasting friendship I treasure and cherish; Sherry, my dream mentor, who was the first to show me the key to unlocking the secrets of my dreams and who has listened to the stories of my heart for more than ten years; Mary, who provided such lovely space in which to dream and grow and heal—you are missed; and all my dreaming friends—past,

Acknowledgments

present and future—who are too numerous to name, but who hold the space in which magic can happen.

To my husband David, my deepest gratitude for your patience and love as I have followed my own path these many years. Thank you for giving me the space to follow my heart, thank you for carrying the weight financially while I did so, and (did I mention?) thanks for being so patient with me. To my mother, I give thanks for the right brain gift of dreaming. To my father, I give thanks for the left brain gifts of analytical and organizational skill. Both gifts were necessary to this project. To my brother Ray, who left us too soon, and to my brother Dick who, for once, didn't follow him on that particular adventure, thanks for being "me big bruddas." My story may be a little "out there" for your taste, but I know you love me anyway! To my sister Christine, thanks for being the best sister with whom I could ever hope to share the load as well as an editor extraordinaire. Thank you, Cameron, for all the gifts you brought into my life and for your "behind-the-scenes" help with the creation of this book. And last, but most definitely not least, my thanks and love to my children, Sarah and Ryan, whose struggles and triumphs I feel as my own. You have given me an opportunity to practice being a better parent as I learn to let go of fear and worry while I watch you blossom and step into your own power.

Prologue

My life changed forever the day my eldest son, Cameron, died at age 26. The last several years of his life had been troubled and our relationship had been sorely tried and tested. His death left many things between us unresolved. The journey of grief and healing that followed this loss took a lot of time, a lot of tears and a lot of self-examination. It was my dark night of the soul, or what I've come to think of as my own personal Ground Zero—the shattering of my known world. Yet, over time, I've come to understand that the greatest tragedy in my life has also been the greatest gift.

Not for one moment do I want you to think that I didn't love my son when I tell you that his death has been the greatest gift I've ever received. Although his death shattered my heart, I know now it was a gift, either from him to me or from the Universe to both of us. And not for one moment do I want you to think that the loss was not the most staggeringly painful experience I've ever had or could imagine. It was. It is. And yet . . .

This is a story of transformation. Since Cameron's death, my life has been an amazing journey into new dimensions of understanding I never dreamed of before. I have journeyed into dreams, into strange and amazing experiences, even into foreign lands. And through it all, I have journeyed deeply into myself.

I believe we each come into this life having a plan for what we want to learn and accomplish. We map out life contracts before we incarnate and we make agreements with others who are coming into the world during our lifetime. Cameron and I surely had a contract with each other. No other explanation makes sense out of the pain and drama we experienced together.

In that other realm where we make these plans, it might be that we are a little overzealous about our goals. We don't always understand all the trials and tribulations fulfilling those contracts and agreements may entail. Our task is complicated by the fact that we arrive here with no conscious knowledge of the

Prologue

content of our contracts. It can be very challenging and difficult to do what we came here to do. That's why, I believe, we keep coming back to try again and again.

For Cameron, I believe death was a release from a painful and no longer useful contract he chose in the time before time. Perhaps he had gotten so far off track that he decided to just start over. But who can say, really, whether he checked out early or simply fulfilled his contract in record time. Whichever the case, I know that he has been able to move on and to find the wholeness and happiness I always wished for him. In truth, despite appearances, he always *was* whole.

For me, his leaving became a gift that helped me to see my own path a little more clearly. Being released from our entanglement and shared drama gave me new freedom in my life. His death was my invitation or initiation into a journey I might otherwise have been too timid, or too preoccupied, to undertake.

This journey has shown me that the bond of love is never broken. We have walked together with those we love before and we shall walk with them again. I believe that although we have been together many times, developing unhealthy karmic connections along the way, we can break through the chains of karma if we choose. We can choose love over drama, love over karma and love over fear. We do not have to wait until our next lifetime together to heal our relationship with a deceased loved one. Death does not sever a relationship; we can continue to meet and interact with those we love even after they have died, especially in our dreams.

My purpose in sharing this story is to show you how grief can become the doorway to awakening. The breaking of your heart can, ultimately, lead you to greater wholeness. The Universe is constantly communicating with us and drawing us forward into better and truer expressions of ourselves. Sometimes it takes the shattering of our known way of being to open our eyes and ears to these messages of hope, healing and growth.

Imagine a leaf floating gracefully down to kiss the surface of a deep still pool, creating gentle ripples that radiate outward. The leaf may appear to be small and alone as it drifts along. But, in truth, it is supported by the vast body of water beneath it. Our lives are a little bit like that leaf. We skim the surface and are tossed about by life's currents. We rarely take the time to look deeper. We begin to imagine the flat plain of that surface existence is all there is, when all the while we are resting upon a deep well of mystery, magic and eternity. As long as we're living the life of a Surface Leaf, we may never tap into our deeper Truth unless something comes along and shatters the surface, pulling us down into a deeper reality. That is the initiation of the Deep Water Leaf.

The death of my son and the personal journey it triggered in my life have allowed me to see, just a little, into the depths of that still pool, beyond the surface of life and death and into a deeper reality. Dreams have been my gateway and synchronicity my guide, while my trusty journal and art supplies have proven to be the most reliable traveling companions imaginable. All of these tools are available to you as well, should you choose to embark on your own transformational journey.

With dreams as my constant companion, amazing opportunities and experiences began to fill my waking life in the months before and the years after my son's death. The dreamspace began to spill over into my waking life. Or perhaps it had always been there and I was just now beginning to notice.

Synchronicity met me at every turn. My life took on the quality of a waking dream at times. And what is synchronicity but a doorway to the dreamspace? Synchronicity allows us to operate within the multidimensional structure of the dreamspace while wide awake.

Somehow Cameron's death broke open a door for me between dreaming and waking, between the living and the dead. It left me standing in a new space with one foot in each world. It opened my eyes to the eternal nature of the soul and the boundlessness of love. Philosophically, I had always understood that death is merely a transition to another state of being, but the loss of Cameron provided a venue for experiencing that truth first hand.

Sharing stories is an ancient human practice. We create and recreate ourselves constantly by the stories we tell. We build

Prologue

community and overcome isolation when we connect to each other through story. When I found an online grief support group[1] about a year after Cameron's death, I became acutely aware of how healing it was for me to hear other people's stories of loss and grief and to share my own story with them. It helped me to see that I was not alone on this journey. Nor are you.

If you are grieving, I wish for you the same kind of healing and transformation that I experienced. It may not be that you lost a child, but everyone experiences life-altering loss and grief at some point in their lives. Even the loss of a job, a home, your health or way of life can trigger immense grief. Yet always, the ending of one stage of life leads to the beginning of the next. If we can recognize even the possibility that within every tragedy a hidden gift awaits our discovery, we can begin to engage meaningfully in the transformative process of grief. Any experience that triggers the shattering of your identity provides you with the opportunity to create a new and better you.

Whatever your journey, whatever brought you to be reading these words today, know that it is no accident. Synchronicity is inviting you to join the Deep Water Leaf Society and embark on your own journey of healing and awakening. If anything in my story resonates within your own heart and soul, consider yourself a member.

The Deep Water Leaf Society

Since childhood, dreams have filled and shaped my life. Sometimes the dreamspace feels more real than waking life and often waking life feels like a dream. Or a nightmare. Where does dreaming leave off and waking begin? What does it mean to wake up, really? How often do we sleepwalk our way through life, missing the extraordinary meaning enfolded in each ordinary moment? It may be that we are more truly awake when we can sense, during our waking hours, the creative magic of the dreamspace all around us.

This is a story about dreaming and about waking up. It is a story about how thin the veil really is between waking and dreaming, between living and dying, between loving and everything else that only masquerades as love. It is a story about letting go and the fullness that comes from doing so.

This is the story of losing my son and finding myself. It begins with a dream. . . .

November 2, 1997 — Deep Water Leaf Society

My four-month-old baby has died. I am filled with grief, utterly devastated.

At the funeral, I come to a decision. I will create the "Deep Water Leaf Society" so that others won't have to go through this same grief. For some reason, that comforts me.

Later, there is something to do with the number seven, and I wake wondering if numbers equal people in my dreams.

Seven equals my sister because she was born in July.

At the time, I had little idea what the dream might be telling me. I only knew that it shook me to my core and left me profoundly sad and profoundly hopeful all at once.

The name, Deep Water Leaf Society, was quite clear in the dream. It puzzled me; it was such an odd phrase. What kind of a club would that be? How could creating it help me to feel better? Why had the number seven come up? And why had I assumed that numbers were people?

After recording the dream in my journal, I reread it and noted that if seven represented my sister, maybe the four-month-old baby represented my eldest son, Cameron (no longer a baby, but a young man of 19) since he was born in April. It gave me an uneasy feeling. Was I destined to lose him?

Lord knows, he'd had a troubled life. He was always doing stupid and dangerous things. He'd been going down a bad path and hanging out with the wrong kind of kids during high school. He'd finally managed to graduate, though, and earlier in the year he'd joined the Marines. While I hoped it would be good for him, I worried about him, too.

As it would turn out, the number seven was both the clue to the identity of the four-month-old and the timeframe in which the dream story would play out in my waking life.

Today I know that this dream was planting the seeds of transformation and healing a full seven years before I would undergo the most tremendously difficult passage in my life: Cameron's death by drug overdose on May 3, 2004.

Cameron's Death

I had a son. Tonight I found a pair of his old, smelly socks in the camper, the last place I saw him before he died. The socks broke my heart all over again.

I can't bring myself to wash them. They stink to high heaven. Lord, that boy's feet stank! He often wore shoes without socks, or wore the same socks for five or six days. When he was on the streets or bouncing from place to place, he didn't always shower regularly. Whenever he'd show up back home to crash for a night or two, that's the first thing that would start to annoy me. "For Christ's sake, Cameron, go wash your feet!" But, truth be told, even after washing them they still stank. I always thought he probably had some kind of disease or infection. Nobody's feet could smell like that otherwise. But his medical care had been beyond the realm of my control for years and so, like so many things, it seemed there was nothing I could do about it.

I try to figure out what to do with them—the socks. I don't want to wash them, but I can't have them stinking up the house. I finally decide to put them with the rest of his clothes in the box in the garage. Then my heart breaks again. He had nothing but the clothes on his back when he died. Well, he didn't even have those at the moment he died, because he was wearing Sheriff Joe's pink boxers and striped jump suit.

He died in the county jail.

~~~

When they came to tell me, they brought me the clothes he was wearing when they arrested him: athletic shorts, baggy jeans, a T-shirt and some old, worn out hiking boots. No socks. He couldn't find them when they came to drag him off to jail, so he went with just the boots on his feet.

All this was in a plastic bag, sealed and tied with a tag bearing his name, inmate number, mug shot and date of birth.

That was all that was left of him. That and those smelly socks.

He'd come home Sunday, the night before he was arrested, asking if he could spend the night here. He knew there was a warrant out for him from the drug mess he'd gotten himself into. He'd tried to turn himself in at the county jail on Saturday night, but when he couldn't produce a picture ID, they wouldn't take him. I don't know where he slept Saturday, but Sunday he showed up at home. I told him he could spend one night, but not in the house. I set him up in the camper and told him in the morning I was going to drive him over to the MVD to get a duplicate driver's license and then drive him back over to the jail so he could turn himself in.

I never got the chance.

~~~

Don't get me started on the "justice" system around here. I'll never be able to figure out why you need a picture ID to turn yourself in, but a posse of five armed lawmen can drag you out of bed on a Monday morning, cuff you and haul you off, no questions asked, no ID required.

They came pounding on the door in the early morning, before eight a.m. Well, I shouldn't say they, because most of them were hiding in case a middle-aged woman wearing nothing but a bathrobe might try to ambush them. Just one of them came to the door. He wasn't wearing a uniform and he looked like a young man around Cameron's age. He smiled and asked, "Is Cameron around?"

Stupid me, I thought he must be a friend of his. I said, "Yeah, but he's still sleeping."

The smile faded and he turned, calling his cohorts out of the woodwork with, "He's here! He's here!"

Next thing I knew, there were five of them shouldering their way right into my house. Then I saw badges and guns. They started to move right on down the hallway toward the bedrooms.

"He's not in here," I said, gesturing toward the arcadia door that led to the backyard where our camp trailer was parked on the RV drive. "He's out in the camper."

Immediately they all changed course and started to push their way past me toward the sliding door.

"Wait a minute! Wait a minute!" I protested. "Just let me wake him up, okay? He's not gonna run. He tried to turn himself in already on Saturday but they wouldn't take him. Please, he's really hard to wake up and you're gonna scare the life out of him. Just let me wake him up. Please!"

I was saying all this as I tried to stay just one step ahead of them. We were all working our way to the arcadia door. The lead guy saw my two Queensland Heelers in the backyard and asked me if they were going to get rowdy. I told him the dogs would probably lick a burglar to death. Just to prove my point, as soon as we got out the door, Cheyenne ran to get her ball and brought it to the lead guy to throw for her. She kept dropping it at his feet every couple of steps, ever optimistic that sooner or later he'd throw it for her. She's crazy about playing catch and completely indiscriminate about with whom she plays.

I was still pleading for them to let me wake Cameron and they finally conceded.

"Can you tell me just one thing," I asked? "Why is it, a kid tries to turn himself in when he's got warrants out, and the damn jail needs to see an ID? He wanted to turn himself in. Why couldn't you just give him that much dignity?"

The lead guy said, "We don't have any control over what the folks down at the jail do. We're just here to do our job. But we'll be sure and let 'em know when we take him in that he tried to turn himself in."

I knew bullshit when I smelled it.

I got to the camper door, opened it and stuck my head in and said, "Cameron, get up. Cameron, you've got to wake up. Now!"

I heard his typical morning grunt of protest. He'd always slept like the dead. I knew that if he was roused too abruptly, he'd immediately startle into fight or flight mode and that would just make everything worse.

"Cameron! You've got to get up!"

That was as much leeway as they were going to give me. I got shouldered out of the way and three of the five pushed their way into the camper to drag him out of bed and order him to get dressed.

Cheyenne was still trying to play ball with one of the cops outside the camper. He was trying to bite back a grin, and I was trying not to cry.

Inside the camper, Cameron couldn't find his socks. He finally said, "Forget it," and shoved his feet into the boots without socks.

They already had him cuffed when they escorted him out the door.

"I'm sorry, Cameron," I said to his back as I trailed them out to the front yard through the RV gate. "Call me when you know which jail you're going to be in."

~~~

On the street in front of the house, all the little kids were walking to school. The neighbors were out, seeing their kids off and picking up their newspapers. Did the police plan the timing of this so it could be the biggest spectacle possible? I watched my son's back and zip-stripped wrists disappear into the police cruiser. The contrast between this bright Monday morning, my silly little ball-playing dog and all of life going on as normal while my son's life was collapsing before my eyes was surreal.

I watched helplessly as five armed men dragged a sleepy and completely cooperative kid, whose only crime was trying to kill himself with drugs, out into the bright morning sun and off to face "justice."

That was the last time I saw my son. I thought at least he'd be safe in jail, but two weeks later, half-way through his 30-day sentence, he was dead. The greatest irony of all: lock up an addict, then let him overdose in jail.

He'd spent the last several years doing crystal meth, selling crystal meth, living on the streets mostly, renting (and trashing) apartments when he could, mooching off of friends, and bouncing into our house when he thought he could get away with it. Every time I picked up the newspaper, I expected to find a story about an unidentified male found dead somewhere and it would be him. So, jail sounded good to me. He wouldn't be able to do drugs in there. He'd have a roof over his head and food to eat.

I figured 30 days in the county jail might be just what he needed.

How wrong could I be?

~~~

I had spoken to him on the phone several times since his arrest, but I hadn't gone to visit him. I figured 30 days would go quickly and I'd had bad experiences with jail visits in the past.

On Sunday evening, two weeks after his arrest, he called me. He sounded self-assured and optimistic as he told me, "Two weeks down, two to go." I told him I'd just ordered some books for him from Amazon and that he should watch for the package. He tried to get me to three-way the call to his girlfriend, but I refused, knowing it was against jail rules. He was disappointed that I wouldn't connect him because his girlfriend's parents would not accept his collect calls from jail. I told him to hang in there and that he'd see her in a couple of weeks. He thanked me for the letter I'd written, and we said goodbye.

I had closed that letter by saying,

> *I surround you with a field of love and protection. I hope that you will use this time to make some decisions and deep inner changes so that your life can be better once you are out. Believe me—you have within you the power to change and the power to make of your life whatever you choose.*

Impulsively, at the bottom of the letter, I'd drawn a little stick figure representation of him surrounded by a spiral and rays of light. In the end, though, my love and protective power were not enough to keep him safe.

The next morning, another bright Monday dawned. I heard the doorbell followed by pounding on the front door. I checked the clock: eight a.m. I was sleepy and annoyed at the disturbance. It was probably the UPS guy or the mailman. Why couldn't they just leave the package on the porch? I tried to go back to sleep.

The pounding continued, insistently. I pulled on my bathrobe and snuck a look out my upstairs bedroom window, which is right above the front porch. Damn. I saw two very official looking men, and they were showing no signs of leaving. I went downstairs and opened the door. I could see by their badges they were from the sheriff's office.

"Ma'am, do you have a son named Cameron Perkins?"

Christ, I thought, *couldn't they leave him alone? What did they think he'd done now? How many times could you arrest a person?*

"Yes," I said, with all the venom I could muster. "He's already in the county jail, why are you looking for him here?"

"Yes, ma'am, we know that. Can we step inside for a moment? Is there anyone else at home with you?"

It still hadn't dawned on me why they were here.

One of them told me his name was Detective Fax, and he introduced his assistant, whose name I have forgotten.

Then he told me my son was dead.

The shock of it hit like an icy dagger in my heart. The blood seemed to drain from me and I fell to the floor with a wail that sounded like it was coming from somewhere in the distance. The tears didn't come right away. There was just a sense of utter disbelief, followed by a certainty that all my life I'd known this day was coming. I just didn't know it would be today. When the finality of it filtered through, the tears began, followed by hiccupping sobs.

I asked them how it happened and they gave me what detail they had. His cellmate had awakened to find him in convulsions in the middle of the night. The guards and medics came right away. They tried to revive him, but he was gone. The cellmate reported that Cameron had been huffing on an asthma inhaler all day.

Detective Fax asked me if Cameron had asthma and I told him no. I told him I imagined he was trying to get high. It crossed my mind to wonder how he got an asthma inhaler. Why would that have been available to him? But I didn't have the presence of mind to ask the question aloud.

Detective Fax asked me if he could call someone to be with me. I told him to call my husband, David.

"But don't tell him on the phone," I pleaded. "I don't want him driving home in a state of shock."

I gave them the office phone number. I heard Detective Fax ask my husband to come home. David wanted to know why, wanted to know if I was okay. Detective Fax told him the news, and I could hear David's strangled cry clear across the room from the phone.

Along with the anguish there was an eerie sense of calm, like the stillness that comes after a devastating storm. Perhaps it was only a blast of endorphins triggered by emotional trauma, but it felt like some kind of window opened up inside of me, giving me a glimpse of incomprehensible peace and light. Even in those first moments of grief, something in me recognized there was a blessing wrapped inside the tragedy. I experienced a kind of release hand in hand with the pain. I felt relief. The drama was over. Cameron didn't have to suffer anymore. None of us did.

Although it would not take long for the light from that window to be dimmed by the darkness of my grief, I knew in that moment that grace was working to grant us all healing at long last.

Cameron's Life

I know the very night he was conceived. It was a summer night in late June 1977. I was 19 years old and had been married about two years, since just after high school graduation. I'd been staying with my parents for a few days of vacation. I'd planned to swim in the pool and just relax, but I was getting bored.

This particular night was stalked by summer storms that circled but never pounced. The night was restless and so was I. I had thought I needed to be away from my husband a little while, but now I found I missed him. I just didn't fit in my childhood home anymore.

So I said, "Screw it." I wrote a note to Mom and Dad telling them I was going home early, and I stuck it on the refrigerator. Around eleven, I hopped in my car and started the hour-and-a-half long drive home from Phoenix to Prescott Valley.

I was high, I think. I don't remember if I smoked up before I got in the car or while I was driving. I had Pink Floyd on, loud. There's that one song, "Time," on the *Dark Side of the Moon* album, about how the days just spin by and all of a sudden you wake up one morning feeling old and wondering where your life went.[2]

And that's the feeling I had inside me those days. The feeling that time was just spinning on without me, while I was getting nowhere. The feeling that I needed to get on with it—whatever "it" was.

I tried to be quiet sneaking into our trailer home. It was after midnight and David got up early for work. I didn't want to wake him, and he wasn't expecting me for a few more days. I tiptoed into our bedroom, but he'd heard me. Only he didn't know it was me. We still joke that if he'd had his shotgun by the bed, he'd have killed me for a robber that night.

As it was, he reached out quicker than a rattlesnake and grabbed me roughly by the wrists. As soon as he figured out it was me and I got my heart swallowed back down, we had to find something to do with all that adrenaline. So we made Cameron. With a start like that, I guess we should have expected he'd be trouble.

~~~

I often wonder what strings Cameron pulled to bring us all together in this lifetime. Looking back, I can sense his hand in it from the start.

My marriage was one of those cases of love at first sight. Except it didn't happen the first time we met. Mutual friends introduced us; my best friend was dating David's best friend, and the Perkins' house was known as *the* place to party most any Friday or Saturday night.

During the summer between my sophomore and junior years in high school, I spent many, many nights there getting wasted. David was just background noise at first, a convenient host. I dated a guy I met there for a couple months and, as I recall, David was seeing someone else at the time as well. I'm not sure what happened to David's main squeeze, but my knight in shining armor dumped me when he learned I wouldn't put out.

One night, David and I both found ourselves unattached, and we finally struck up a conversation. David asked me if I wanted to go outside and meet the goose. I told him, "That's the stupidest pickup line I've ever heard." He insisted that there really was a pet goose outside, so I followed him, out of curiosity.

We found the goose near the living room window, getting high on the smoke wafting out through the open screen and bobbing his head to the loud rock music. A party goose! Who knew?

We climbed onto the hood of an old car in the yard and stared up at the stars. Something in the clear night air sucked the cobwebs out of our brains and we looked at each other as if for the first time. There was instant chemistry and we kissed. I knew that very moment he was the one. It was like I'd never really looked at him before. So it *was* love at first sight. I'd just been blind for a while.

I wonder now if Cameron wasn't up there, in soul form, shouting, "Finally! What took you guys so long?!" I think he was anxious to be born, to work something out with us. I think that he'd been waiting a long, long time for all of us to be in the same place at the same time.

~~~

It took a few more years for us to marry and finally bring Cameron into our lives. As soon as I learned I was pregnant, my whole life changed. It was as if I grew up overnight. I quit smoking cigarettes, stopped smoking pot, and curbed my drinking a lot. In those days, we weren't told to quit drinking (at least, I was never told to) and I didn't realize it could be dangerous for the baby if I drank in moderation. I had been a wild teenager, a real party girl, but now all I could think about was being a mom. In retrospect, I wonder how much my lifestyle, before and during pregnancy, may have affected Cameron's development.

His due date was April 7th, but he must have been in a hurry. He nearly set himself up for a lifetime of teasing and torment by sending me into labor on April Fools' Day. He was spared that fate by an excruciatingly long labor, tempered in the final hours by a dose of Demerol that knocked me into a different universe. He finally arrived (assisted by forceps, as I'd long since lost the strength to push) in the early morning hours of April 2, 1978.

He was born with an insatiable appetite for attention and a fearless, boundless sense of curiosity that bordered on suicidal. He was born with ADHD, Attention Deficit/Hyperactive Disorder.

Oh, I didn't know all that at the time. He was my firstborn, so I had no basis for comparison. He was a wanted and well-loved baby who did nothing but cry and nurse for the first six months of his life. Sleep was something that happened in fits and starts and never lasted for long. He was four months old before he slept through the night—and a short night at that. I was lucky if he would sleep until 4:00 or 4:30 in the morning. All the various "experts" had their take on it.

"It's just colic," my mother advised. "It will pass."

"Let him cry," said my mother-in-law, "you'll spoil him if you pick him up every time he cries."

"Nothing but breast milk for the first six months," insisted the pediatrician.

"Feed him some cereal before bed," my mother-in-law countered.

I was twenty years old. I didn't know *nothin' 'bout birthin' babies*, much less raising them. But none of these experts knew anything about what it was like living with this child.

Eventually he outgrew the non-stop crying and started to sleep through the night and nap in the day, and we settled into our lives together.

I loved that child with all my heart. He was such a beautiful little boy, his deep brown eyes always sparkling with curiosity and mischief. He had the longest, blackest eyelashes. He could be so loving, snuggling in my lap for hugs and tickles. He was smart and clever and funny. It hurts me to think that the simple joys we had (and we did have them) have been so overshadowed in my mind by the painful memories of the difficult times that seemed to fill his life.

We didn't have speed-dial in those days, but if we'd had it, Poison Control would have been first on the list in our house. I quickly learned you could baby-proof a house, but you couldn't Cameron-proof it. He was curious and into everything. If there was something dangerous within 100 yards, including straight up, he'd find it: metal objects to put into electrical outlets, precarious heights from which to leap, arthritis rub to put in his mouth.

He didn't outgrow it, and he wasn't content to be the only subject of his lab experiments, either. I once walked into his baby sister's room to find that he had filled her ears with diaper rash cream and thoroughly powdered her head. Thank goodness he didn't take the next logical step and cover her face with a disposable diaper, blocking off her ability to breathe!

At the age of five, he nearly drowned in a lake near our Spokane, Washington, home. We'd gone for a nice summer day of relaxing fun with a neighbor and her children. I had turned my back for just a second to stir up some Kool-Aid for the kids. I turned around and asked, "Where's Cameron?"

Just like in the movies, everything seemed to go into slow-motion as the panic bubbled up in me. Someone pointed out into the lake and shouted, "There!" I spotted an empty inner tube bobbing in the water and ran toward it.

I found him under the waist-deep water, grabbed him around the belly, and ran back to the shore. When I pulled him from the water, his lips were turning blue and he was unconscious. I don't know if he was still breathing or not, but apparently my instinctual Heimlich-style grip just beneath his rib cage revived him. When I sprinted out of the lake with Cameron clutched under my arm, it was as though I'd applied a kind of accidental CPR. By the time we got to shore and I put him on a blanket, he was sitting up, talking and laughing, excitedly telling me all about the fish he saw under the water.

When he started kindergarten that fall, the teacher called me to say she'd never in her fifteen years of teaching seen a child as overactive as Cameron. This was the first inkling I had that maybe this wasn't normal, average, kids-will-be-kids behavior. Maybe we needed to find out what was going on with him. My family doctor suggested it might be Attention Deficit Disorder (ADD). This was a fairly new idea in 1983, not the rampant, epidemic diagnosis that it is today.

"Let's try Ritalin," the doctor said.

So we did, on and off, for the next five years. In some ways it helped, but in others it made things worse; it was like making a choice between having my child be a live missile with no guidance system or a zombie with headaches and moodiness. If you look on the Internet today, you'll find article after article about Ritalin, its side effects and the rampant over-prescription of this drug to children who are labeled with ADD and ADHD. Given the same choice today, I wouldn't put my child on Ritalin, but at the time it seemed wise to follow my doctor's advice. Unfortunately, the Ritalin never curbed Cameron's tendency to make poor choices.

Cameron's Life

As a young boy, he wouldn't dream of backing down on a dare. He once ingested castor beans (the source of the deadly poison, Ricin) at the instigation of a neighbor boy who told him they were pinto beans and dared him to eat them raw. After he ate them, the boy panicked and told him they weren't pinto beans and his mamma had told him never to eat the beans off that bush because they were poisonous. The episode triggered one of our many childhood trips to the emergency room. Cameron, under protest, was forced to down a bottle of liquid charcoal to absorb the poison in his system.

In elementary school, Cameron was the proverbial square peg in a round hole; he just didn't fit in the system. The Ritalin kept him toned down a notch, but he still couldn't (or wouldn't) play the game by the rules.

Creative and intelligent, he'd find his own way around boring chores like in-class worksheets or homework. In first grade, he figured out that while the papers were being passed forward from the back of each row, he could erase the smart kid's name from an A-quality paper and replace it with his own.

He became a masterful storyteller, which is really a euphemism for pathological liar. When he did something wrong and got caught, he would never tell the real story. He'd begin with complete denial, then, as evidence was produced, he'd cop to as minimal a part of the crime as he thought he could get away with. He didn't eat *all* of the cookies; he ate only *one*. The bag was almost empty when he found it. Someone else must have eaten the rest. Or, he didn't take *all* of the money from his sister's piggy bank; he borrowed only *a quarter*. She must have spent the rest.

I think he ended up believing his stories more than the reality of whatever he'd done. He never seemed to learn from his mistakes or their consequences. He never seemed able to relate the consequences to his actions in a cause-and-effect way. And the size of the trouble he got into grew right along with him.

~~~

During his school years, he became moody and impossible to control. Adolescence was filled with individual and family therapy. Cameron never wanted to accept that he wasn't "normal." Who could blame him? What *is* normal, anyway?

Today he'd be called an Indigo Child, one of those special children thought to be the first in a new wave of human evolution, but in the '80s I'd never heard of the concept.

Some people think that children who are labeled with ADD, ADHD and other behavioral dysfunctions, as well as kids who exhibit extraordinary traits such as enhanced psychic abilities, may be the front runners of a more advanced human species. Unfortunately, these kids often struggle in life because they don't fit into the status quo. We don't know what to make of them or what to do with them. Their way of being collides with the world's expectations.

But Indigos are extremely intelligent, despite any appearance of disability or dysfunction. Cameron was so smart that he figured out the therapists right away; he told them what they wanted to hear during sessions and then came home without changing his behavior in the least.

Our home became a constant battleground. Anything that felt like a rule or a restriction, Cameron ignored on principle. Chores, homework, curfew and bedtime chafed, and Cameron resisted them with all his might. Punishments like no TV or being grounded simply fed the anger and sullenness that were always simmering just below the surface.

At the age of twelve, during one miserable year when we lived in Las Vegas, he ran away from home and spent the night out in the desert with a friend. I don't believe I had ever felt such panic. As I paced the floor in our apartment while the police and my husband searched for him, I wrote a letter to him in my journal.

> *I hope that you never have to experience what I'm going through (or worse) with any of your own children. Indeed, I hope you live long and fully enough to have children of your own — sometimes I am truly afraid you won't... You are out there somewhere in the desert. You're probably COLD and HUNGRY and THIRSTY. Maybe even hurt . . . And you <u>chose</u> to be there*

instead of here. That existence is preferable to the torture of living with us—with <u>me</u>. I don't understand how this has all gone so wrong.

The following day he was found, safe and no worse for the wear. Dirty and tired, he returned home, sullen and unrepentant. After this experience, I took him in for evaluation and testing with a psychiatrist. The pressure of the testing, the implication that something was really wrong with him, pushed him over the edge for a time. The night before the final round of tests, I found him slicing the bottom of his feet with a jagged, broken plastic protractor. I guess he was acting out his self-loathing and trying to turn all his inner pain into something physical, something that could be seen. He may as well have been slicing up my heart, because I could feel every stroke as I raced across the room to take that unlikely weapon away from him.

The next day, after the battery of psychological tests was completed, an official diagnosis of ADHD was confirmed. Cameron scored in the genius range on the IQ test, but was nearly dysfunctional in the world in which he lived. Well, now we had a name for it, but we were no closer to a solution.

Nothing much changed after the diagnosis. We started a new round of counseling, but he already knew how to play that system. He didn't want to change, didn't want to accept a label like ADHD, didn't want to go on meds, didn't want to play by society's rules. He was playing his own game.

As a teenager, he began to hang out with gang-bangers. He started drinking and doing drugs. I wasn't completely aware of all that was going on at the time; Cameron was really good at covering his tracks and he had an answer for every question about what he was up to. Looking back I realize there were lots of signs, like the industrial-style markers I kept finding in his room. Those heavy duty permanent markers were obvious tools for graffiti and also produced strong enough fumes for huffing (one of the first ways kids learn to get high). He rarely brought his friends around the house, preferring to go out to meet them. Hindsight tells me I should have paid more attention, but truthfully, I probably didn't want to know. I had blinders on and

I preferred to attribute his bad attitude and behavior to the ADHD.

So, I didn't know all the details, but I knew things were getting bad. His behavior was getting worse and worse. There were lots of arguments, groundings, threats and punishments. None of it mattered. He'd just sneak out in the middle of the night and do whatever he damn well pleased.

He was skipping school all the time, failing classes. Detentions and suspensions were becoming commonplace. He wouldn't contribute at all around the house with chores and he would not even try to be civil to any of us.

None of the "effective parenting" or disciplinary strategies we'd learned through counseling and taking classes seemed to work with Cameron. With patience growing thinner by the day, tough love seemed the only option.

When he was in high school, I gave him a choice: start doing his share around the house or get a job and pay rent to live with us. I wasn't interested in the money. I just wanted him to wake up and engage, be a part of the family, be decent to his siblings, be responsible for himself. He chose the rent, but then never paid it. So that just became another on-going argument.

I finally gave him an ultimatum: go to school every day and follow some minimal rules at home or move out. He moved out. He was only 16. I felt so guilty, like such a terrible mother. I'd thrown down the gauntlet and he'd called my bluff. He bounced around from friend to friend, and after some time, maybe six months, he came back home.

He barely finished high school, but finally got his diploma by going to night school. At 19, he joined the Marines. We all breathed a sigh of relief. Surely *that* would straighten him out. It would be just the discipline he needed. He'd develop a sense of responsibility and he'd learn what it meant to rely on people and to have them rely on him. I don't think I was ever prouder of him (or he of himself) than the day he graduated from boot camp.

But the glow tarnished pretty quickly. Faced with the 24-hour-a-day, in your face structure of the Corps plus the long spells of boredom when there wasn't any demanding training going on,

Cameron's Life

Cameron started drinking heavily. And when he drank, all his anger came out. He would get into fist fights with anyone over nothing at all. Eventually, he decked a superior officer and it was all over for him. He faced a court martial, spent some time in the brig and was discharged for bad conduct after three years of service.

From that point on he was at loose ends. Unable or unwilling to hold a steady job, he spent a couple of years basically living on the streets. He started using crystal meth.

My husband, David, who owns a concrete company, gave him several chances to work full time and learn the business, but Cameron kept blowing it off for one reason after another. He once told me he'd rather dumpster-dive and panhandle than demean himself by digging footings and setting stems like any other simple laborer when his father owned the company.

My heart broke daily as I watched Cameron self-destruct. Life became a roller coaster of bailing him out of trouble, loaning him money, letting him come back home, and then kicking him out again. I could not have his drugs, guns and dangerous lifestyle in my home, yet I couldn't stand to think of him on the streets with nowhere to turn. I knew he needed to go into rehab. I'd have been willing to pay for it if I thought he was ready to realize he needed help. I didn't think rehab would do any good if he was forced into it. He'd just go back to his old habits once he got out.

I had two other children who were growing up to be loving, responsible, functional young adults, and I didn't want his influence ruining that. I had a loving husband who had long since let go of the notion that we could control or change Cameron. I had not yet figured that out and found it desperately difficult to let go. It was 2002 and Cameron was 24 years old. Although he was a young adult, he was still my little boy. I worried about him constantly and lived in a state of waiting for the next shoe to drop. I needed to find a way to distance myself from the constant drama his life had become.

Turtle Soup

The Creative Journal Expressive Arts program, developed by Lucia Capacchione, Ph.D.,[3] is one of the many synchronistic opportunities that arrived at just the right time to prepare me for and help me through the loss that was to come.

I found the program as I was searching for the next step in my life and work. Reaching a stage of total burnout, I had left my career in computer programming in the late '90s. I was tired of working for a paycheck instead of doing something I could be passionate about. I was very interested in the connections between science and spirituality, the implications of quantum physics, and consciousness as a creative force. I returned to school and completed an interdisciplinary studies degree in religious studies and philosophy, with an emphasis on bridging science and spirituality.

As I was gearing up for final exams and graduation at the end of 2002, my mother became very ill. She was diagnosed with kidney failure and was put on dialysis. During the first part of 2003, I was deeply involved in caring for her, so I didn't make much progress on developing a new career path. As the summer of 2003 arrived, I was determined to get back on track with creating my future.

The work that most interested me revolved around human development and potential. I wanted to find an avenue through which I could teach people how to follow their hearts to find fulfillment in life. The teacher always teaches what she herself seeks to find.

I stumbled across Dr. Capacchione's work when I found her book, *Visioning: Ten Steps to Designing the Life of Your Dreams*[4] during the summer of 2003. The amazing process outlined within the book combines the art of collage with journaling to create a powerful, tangible, organized path for activating the Law of Attraction, which says that we attract into our lives the things upon which we focus. I was determined to follow the steps in the book to create a vision for my own future.

When synchronicities appear in my life, I've learned to tune in. It is the Universe's way of getting my attention and signaling that I'm on the right path.

Just before I created my first Visioning®5 collage, I had a powerful dream.

May 20, 2003 -- Turtle Soup

I'm sitting on top of a box. There is a turtle inside and I think about catching him to make soup. But the turtle is pushing up on the lid of the box trying to get out and it's scaring me. I'm afraid to reach in. I am calling for someone to help me get the turtle. They are telling me to just reach in and grab it. But I am afraid. If I get off the top of the box, he'll come right after me and devour me. I get very scared and start yelling for help. I wake up yelling.

My thoughts after the dream were that something in me was boxed in—something that I was both drawn to (wanting to make soup, which would nourish me) and terrified of (will I eat the turtle, or will it eat me?). I thought this had to do with the real me wanting to follow where my heart would lead despite all the practical considerations of income and security. Was I ready to walk the talk? Or was I willing to stay in the box of status quo and comfort zones?

Two days after the Turtle Soup dream I began to gather magazine photos and phrases for my first collage. The very first magazine I picked up was an old issue of *Science & Spirit*. Opening the magazine at random, I saw an article titled "God, Physics and Turtle Soup."[6] I was delighted and intrigued to see the theme of turtle soup begin to repeat itself. The photo of the turtle from that article became a part of my collage. I placed him coming from behind a tri-fold screen that I labeled with the phrase, "Out of the Box."

There was much more to the collage, of course. All of it focused on my vision for my future life's work. It included images of teaching, writing books, working from the heart, opening to Spirit and finding success, joy and fulfillment.

I spent a long time on this first collage—much longer, I would learn, than is necessary or even desirable. I was pretty stuck in my left brain, analyzing every image and word, laying things out in little disconnected groups. The process is meant to take no more than a day, and can be done easily in as little as two hours. As I've worked with Visioning® over time, I've discovered it's more effective to work fast and let the images guide you rather than the other way around. It is meant to be a truly right-brained, organic process. At any rate, I spent about a week, a few hours each day, completing my first vision.

The day that I finished the collage, the Daily Guide entry in my *Science of Mind* magazine told a fable about a man named Chuang-tse, who was relaxing by the river one day when one of the king's men came along and invited him to take an important, prestigious and well-paid position at the castle of the king. Chuang-tse asked the messenger if it was true that the king had a rare 2000-year-old tortoise that he kept in a silk-lined box in the castle. The messenger said it was true. Chuang-tse then asked the messenger whether he thought the tortoise would be happier in the silk-lined box or wallowing in a mud hole. The messenger replied, in the mud, of course! Chuang-tse told the messenger to leave him alone, because he would rather flap his own tail in the mud than be trapped in the castle. Thanks, but no thanks to the job![7]

So, here was the turtle again, encouraging me to get out of the box and stay out of it. With a trilogy of turtles in a week's time, I knew that I must be on the right track.

The Visioning® process was amazing. The collage I created gave me such a feeling of clarity and excited expectation for the road ahead. After using the book to create my first collage, I knew this would make a terrific workshop that could empower everyone it reached. It was exactly the kind of work I would love to teach.

I searched for more information about Dr. Capacchione, the author, and found she offered a certification program called Creative Journal Expressive Arts (CJEA): an intense year of study to train and certify instructors in all of her expressive arts and journaling techniques. This was an impressively broad body of work that went far beyond the single process of Visioning®. All of the processes were geared toward self-discovery, personal growth and healing. I knew right away I had found the next step on my path and I signed up for the first available start date, which was October of 2003.

A few months after I completed this first collage, Cameron was arrested on charges of selling crystal meth to an undercover agent. The sale had actually taken place almost a year before, but that's the way undercover operations work. They want to follow the trail as far as it will take them before blowing their cover.

Even though Cameron had been trying to turn his life around (he'd moved into a halfway house and was attending Narcotics Annonymous meetings) his past was about to catch up with him. Crystal meth is classified as a dangerous substance, and rightly so; it is one of the most addictive drugs out there. Cameron was charged with selling crystal meth in an amount three times the threshold level, making his offense a Class 2 Felony. Even as a first offense, that could carry a very hefty sentence. For now, he was in the county jail awaiting arraignment and trial.

Visiting a child in the county jail is no picnic. It is one of the most demeaning and heartbreaking things I've ever done. Sheriff Joe Arpaio, the Sheriff of Maricopa County and overseer of the county's jails, has gained national notoriety as the toughest sheriff in America. He prides himself on dressing prisoners in pink boxers, feeding them green bologna and housing them in tents. This was the system in which Cameron now found himself.

There is no sense of human dignity there. It is as if simply being *charged* with a crime is enough to strip you of all your rights. The idea that one is assumed innocent until proven guilty is a myth. Being related to someone "inside" means you are just as bad. Waiting to get in for a visit can take hours. You have to remove all of your jewelry and dress according to a strict dress code: no sleeveless or low cut blouses, no shorts or short skirts. You get to sit across a table from your inmate, but no touching is allowed. Guards are posted all around the visitation room and your conversation is monitored.

I only visited twice. I just couldn't handle it. If it was this hard just visiting, I couldn't imagine what it must be like being detained inside.

At first we thought it best not to post bail for Cameron. We thought that maybe he needed to stew in his own juices for a while and really think about what a mess he'd made of his life. But we learned that the court system moves very slowly. If he had to stay in jail until his sentencing, it could be six months or more.

After attending some of his preliminary hearings, I also became aware of how differently a judge looks at an inmate in a jumpsuit and handcuffs versus someone in street clothes facing the same charges. Eventually we put our house up as collateral and posted bail.

In the months of summer and early fall, I had dream after worrying dream about Cameron: Cameron being chased by the police, Cameron hiding in a crawlspace, Cameron accidentally shooting himself in the head. There were other dreams that I didn't relate to Cameron that may have been warning me just the same, like the one where I started out on a journey from an airport and ended up bringing flowers to a funeral.

I *was* just beginning a journey, a journey to personal freedom and authenticity. It is sadly ironic that just as I began to climb out of my box, Cameron was sinking ever deeper into a box from which he would never escape. Somehow my freedom and his bondage were all entangled. Both my freedom and his would come with the price of his death.

Was that the only way it could have happened? I don't know. I only know that's how it did happen.

Interestingly, one of the images in that first collage showed a winding pathway with a big, black chasm breaking through the path about halfway to the glowing light at the end of the journey. At the top of the image, I had glued the phrase "Eyes on the Prize."

At the time it meant to me that I might encounter some obstacles on the way to my destination, but that I could choose to persevere and keep my eyes on the goal. Looking at it now I see yet another precognition of the very dark journey awaiting me, a journey that would begin with Cameron's death, which would occur almost exactly half way through my CJEA training year.

When I look at that image now, it is the word "ReVision" that jumps out at me. Cameron's death would lead me, over time, to look at *everything* differently.

The Blessing of Padre Pio

I was raised Catholic, although it has been more than three decades since I have practiced that early faith actively. During my teenage years, I rebelled. I saw more hypocrisy and greed than truth within the structure of my religious upbringing.

Perhaps it was simply the rebelliousness of youth, or perhaps it was a necessary step in my own personal evolution. At any rate, I began by throwing out the baby with the bathwater. Literally. I disowned the baby Jesus. I rejected the entire notion of Jesus as Savior, a holy child who came and suffered on our behalf. I rejected the notion of original sin, rejected the notion of some privileged class of priests who could intervene for me before God. Furthermore, I rejected God himself and washed my hands once and for all of all that religious hogwash. I didn't need it. I vowed not to subject my own children to such rigid dogma. I would allow them to choose for themselves.

For perhaps ten years or longer, I remained content with that decision, but as I grew into adulthood, married, started a family and began a career, I found there was an empty space in me, an undefined longing for something more. I experimented, on and off, with various practices—meditation, yoga, this church or that—never quite finding that elusive connection to the greater whole I sensed was there.

Eventually I discovered the New Thought movement, a branch of religion or spirituality that embraces the power of positive thinking and recognizes humans as co-creators with a panentheistic God. I found the Unity Church, and that became my spiritual home for a time. It gave me a liberating perspective on my own spiritual power as it encouraged direct communion with Spirit, no priesthood required. For me, it seemed to strip away all the layers of dogma leaving a refreshingly pure and innocent experience of faith. Unity taught me that I was in control of my own destiny. I could tap into the Universal Power of creation and, with my thoughts, words and attitudes, create my own reality.

Despite the gradual metamorphosis in my spiritual beliefs and practices, I have grown to value the contribution that my early religious upbringing gave me. I often thank Catholicism for infusing me with a sense of the divine and immortal nature of life. While today my faith takes a very different form than that original Catholic tradition, Catholicism instilled in me an unshakable belief in a Higher Power and faith that good will triumph over evil, at least over the long haul.

To this day I have a nostalgic longing for the comfort I once found in the church of my childhood. Although I rejected the structure of Catholicism, I'm still drawn to the architecture and tangible sacredness of the building itself: the immense space, the great domed roof reaching up into the heavens, the quality of light streaming through the stained glass windows, the lingering scent of incense, the echoing of my shoes on the marble floor, the cool smoothness of the polished wooden pews, the palpable sense of decades of prayers offered, heard and answered.

While the image of Jesus on the cross is one to which I've not yet reconciled, there is another icon of Catholicism that has remained curiously close to my heart: Mary, the Holy Mother. In times of great distress or fear, I have found myself reciting the Hail Mary automatically and without conscious thought. Each time I've experienced this automatic response, I have shaken my head and wondered at how deeply rooted, how in the blood, my early training lies, despite years of attempting to distance myself from it. I try to dismiss the inclination to cling to this ritual prayer as nothing more than ingrained habit. Yet, beyond the habitual response, there lies a great comfort and a great feeling of connection to that deeper dimension of Spirit as I recite the words.

As Cameron became ever more deeply enmeshed in his drug-induced dysfunction, I grew ever wearier and desperate for change. In the late summer of 2003, Cameron was working his way through the slow meanderings of the court system. He was out on bail awaiting trial or a plea agreement. He'd moved into a halfway house and was working day labor jobs while looking for a better opportunity.

It was tough for him to try and pull himself out of the deep hole he'd created. He now had an address at the halfway house, but previously he'd been living on the streets. He had no phone, no recent work history, no decent clothes and pending criminal charges. Not many people were willing to give him a chance. Even though he had been working hard to control his addiction and turn his life around, we had been advised to expect a seven to ten year sentence in the state prison. His public defender was trying to negotiate a reduced sentence through a plea agreement. I was holding my breath.

In every waking moment, I was recognizing the need for breaking whatever karmic bonds held us trapped in this never ending drama. I had lived so many years in a codependent state, like a puppet constantly having my strings pulled by the events in Cameron's life. We were so entangled that sometimes I didn't know where his life left off and mine began. I was always trying on the one hand to keep my son alive and healthy and out of harm's way, and on the other hand to tame the fearful and sometimes viciously recriminating voice in me that was so ready to lash out at him in judgment. I would bounce between being his rescuer and being his judge and jury.

I had reached the breaking point in what seemed a lifetime of trying to rescue my wayward child. The thought of him spending years in prison was heartbreaking, yet I knew it was through his own choices that he'd arrived in this place. Whatever mistakes I may have made raising him, he was a grown man now and needed to stand on his own two feet, make his own decisions, and suffer the consequences for those decisions.

For months, I had been praying for the ability to let go. Rather than praying for any specific outcome, my prayer had become simply for him to be whole and happy and for me to be able to step out of the habitual role of rescuing.

One midweek summer day, I found myself near St. Francis Xavier, my childhood church, and I decided to stop and step inside to see if any peace could be found there. The church was deserted except for the organist who was practicing various pieces of music.

I wandered around and looked in all the little alcoves, their candles perpetually lit in prayer before statues of various saints. The candles are electric now; a few coins in the slot and the push of a button can send one's prayers speeding out for handling the modern way. Maybe soon there will be email and text-messaging options.

I sat in the center of the church and looked up into the dome. Its little diamond-shaped blue stained glass windows had always felt to me like stars in the sky. I closed my eyes and recognized that I no longer knew how to pray or to whom. I moved to sit in front of the statue of Mary in the front of the church, to the left of the altar and the pulpit.

I talked to Mary, one mother to another. How had she been able to bear the pain of losing her son? How would I bear losing mine to prison? I prayed a few Hail Marys and I closed my eyes and cried. I asked Mary to heal my son and to heal my heart. I cried about our broken world and all the broken people in it. I asked her to make me a good mother and to help Cameron, to make him whole again. I sat quietly for a few minutes, trying not to cry anymore.

I don't know what I believe, really, about Mary and Jesus and all that, but I do believe in the love of a mother for her child, and I believe there is Something that feels our tears and broken hearts. I thanked Mary for listening. I felt she could understand in a way that only a mother who has seen her own child suffer could.

As I sat at Mary's feet, the organist had been practicing odd bits of music, but nothing I recognized. I got ready to leave and he began to play Greensleeves: "What child is this who laid to rest, on Mary's lap is sleeping . . .?" A Christmas carol in August? I think Mary was holding Cameron in her heart just then. It gave me an odd feeling of comfort.

That night, I dreamed about receiving a blessing.

> ### August 26, 2003 — The Blessing of Father Pio
>
>
>
> *A man comes to bless us. He stops and asks me, "Whose blessing would you like, Father Pio's?" I shrug. I have not asked for a blessing and I'm not sure I believe in blessings anyway. He says, "Yes, Father Pio, I think." He cups his hands and pours water over my head—so much water that the blanket over my chest gets soaked, for I am suddenly in my bed. I take the blessing somewhat sullenly.*
>
> *Later, I can't get Father Pio out of my mind. I hear there is a book about his life and I go to the library to find it. The librarian has the book and she's reading the back flap. She says, "This can't be! The flap says it's an incredibly popular best seller." She is surprised that a story about an obscure saint would be so popular. But I tell her, no, it is a very great story. The book opens from top to bottom instead of side to side—like a secretary's spiral notebook.*

I woke from this dream feeling I had truly been blessed. It felt disorientingly real, and I half expected to find my bed sheets soaked. The name Father Pio stuck in my head and would not let go. Although I had never heard the name, I felt that it was the name of a real person and that I probably *could* find his life story in a book somewhere. After my visit to the church and my prayers to Mary, I felt as though this Father Pio might be a patron saint for Cameron or for me or for both of us. Within the dream, I didn't really accept the blessing—I was rather standoffish about it. But when I awoke, it felt like a true gift.

After recording my dream, I went directly to the Internet to search for Father Pio. I learned that there was, indeed, a real person by the name of Padre Pio, a Capuchin priest who had lived in Italy and reputedly experienced the stigmata—the wounds of Christ. He is credited with a number of miracles and was canonized by the Catholic Church in June of 2002.

The day after my dream of Padre Pio's blessing, Cameron called to tell me that his public defender had contacted him with a plea offer: 90 days, a $2500 fine, and three years probation. His attorney thought the judge might even defer the jail time. A deferred sentence would mean that unless Cameron violated the terms of his probation he would serve no time at all. Padre Pio's blessing had turned into a small miracle. Cameron had been given an amazing second chance.

I went to the library and checked out some books about Padre Pio. I learned that he was devoted to the Virgin Mary and often interceded for people at her request. I learned that he empathized deeply with those who were imprisoned. I learned that he had appeared to others in dreams and that his miracles were not limited strictly to good practicing Catholics.[8] I believe that Mary sent Padre Pio to me in answer to my prayers.

One humorous incident from his life, more than anything else, confirmed to me that my dream had been real. At one point in Padre Pio's life, he blessed and cured a woman who had been blind. Ecstatic, she fell at his feet begging over and over again for his blessing. He told her to get up, that he had already blessed her, but she kept repeating, "Bless me, Padre. Bless me." Exasperated, he finally said to her, "What kind of blessing do you want? A pail of water on your head?"[9]

I had to chuckle when I thought about my dream, in which he had poured so much water over my head that my bed was soaked. I felt that beyond the miracle of Cameron's generous plea offer, I was being asked to be grateful for all the amazing gifts I had in my life. Instead of begging to be blessed, like the once-blind woman, it was time to open my eyes to the blessings all around me every day.

And a huge, life-saving blessing was about to come my way through the CJEA training I would begin in October.

Saying Goodbye

Just a few days before my first CJEA training intensive, I had an eerie dream.

> ### October 4, 2003 — Brain Adjustment
>
>
>
> *They are going to open up our heads and do a brain procedure. Some brains will be completely removed. Others will be adjusted. Some will be switched and partially switched with others. We have no choice about the procedure and it is time to do it now. Some of us will die.*

I had a vague feeling that Cameron was part of this dream. I felt that both Cameron and I were going to have the brain procedure. It seemed risky, but it also seemed like it might be our only hope. I would soon find out that the year of CJEA training would be all about quieting the left brain, opening up the right brain and creating more communication and balance between the two hemispheres. My brain was definitely in for some major adjusting!

Cameron's brain, in the meantime, may have already been permanently damaged by the crystal meth. His behavior was irrational and often paranoid. Incredibly, he was not sure he should take the plea agreement. He didn't want to risk the 90 days jail time because it might mess up his relationship with his girlfriend. I couldn't believe he was serious. He was guilty and the evidence would prove it. Why would he risk a trial with a potential sentence of seven to ten years when he could do 90 days and be done with it? I felt as though if anyone's brain needed adjusting, his certainly did.

And the dream ended with the ominous warning that some of us would die. Little did I know at the time that Cameron *would* die before the end of my training year.

I arrived in beautiful Cambria, California for the first week of training excited to learn all I could. While I had signed up with the intention of creating a teaching practice that would help others, I soon learned the first rule of the program: you can't take someone else where you haven't been yourself. It was mandatory that all students do their own journaling and expressive arts work, healing whatever called for healing in themselves.

The tools and practices I learned were immediately applicable to my struggles with Cameron as well as my own life path. I learned to recognize and process my emotions, listen to the voice of my Inner Child, tune into the wisdom of my Higher Self, and visualize and express the things that were blocking my forward motion. The work introduced me to a whole cast of characters that live inside me. It helped me to become more conscious of my decisions rather than always acting out of habitual response, under the direction of an out of control critical, perfectionist voice. I discovered that my Inner Nurturer, whose role was supposed to be taking care of my own Inner Child, was completely turned outward, trying to take care of everyone else and especially trying to "fix" Cameron.

The journaling, which included lots of drawing as well as writing with both hands, was extremely enlightening and helped me to begin to change my relationship with Cameron. Ninety percent of my energy and attention had been wrapped up in the things that were going on in *his* life. I needed to find balance and begin to reclaim my own life. During that first week of training, I had a dream about a child.

October 14, 2003 — The Blue Child

I see children and they are all different colors—rainbow colors, not normal skin colors. There is one that is a beautiful blue—sort of a bright aqua blue. This child really calls to me— like I want to help it and it wants me to.

After the dream I wondered whether the child was Cameron or my own sad little Inner Child. I suspected the latter, since the dream child appeared in my favorite color turquoise. I was learning that in the process of trying to help Cameron all the time, and in the process of watching him suffer, my own Inner Child was in deep distress. It felt selfish at first, but I knew that if I didn't start nurturing myself, I would eventually become ill or go crazy.

Expressive arts work is very helpful in recovery from addiction, and one of Dr. Capacchione's books, *Recovery of Your Inner Child*, has been used in treatment centers around the world to help people recovering from abuse and addiction. The premise of the book is that we can overcome the traumas of our past if we learn to develop a strong Protective Parent and a strong Nurturing Parent within ourselves. We can reparent our Inner Child and break free from the past and whatever we feel might have been missing in our childhood.[10]

This was such a hopeful thought for me. I had felt as though any of the mistakes I might have made as a parent were permanent and irreparable. Maybe they weren't. Maybe Cameron could learn to reparent himself.

The CJEA training was helping me to recognize family dynamics and patterns in my own behavior that may have contributed to Cameron's problems. I had constantly run interference and stepped in whenever I thought David was being too hard on Cameron, when maybe an extra firm hand was exactly what he needed. At any rate, whether David *was* being too hard on him or not, my stepping in only showed Cameron that he could play one of us off the other.

Then there was my own waffling back and forth between coming down hard and bailing him out. Instead of making him accept responsibility for his own behavior from the very beginning, I'd always come back (in my own mind) to using the ADHD as an excuse. And by doing so, I taught Cameron to use it as an excuse as well. Granted, ADHD makes life difficult, but if you suffer from it you still have to learn how to live with it and function in the world, whether that means taking medication or just learning how to work with it.

I felt that alcohol, which was a fixture in our household, was another factor in Cameron's dysfunction. Both David and I used alcohol as a means of relaxation, recreation and de-stressing. While neither of us was an alcoholic in the sense of being physically addicted, drinking to the extreme of blackouts, or becoming irresponsible or unproductive in our lives, beer and wine were a constant presence in our home. Drinking was part of the fabric of life, as it had been in the homes in which we grew up. Having a drink was synonymous with fun and happiness. What this modeled for Cameron and our other two kids was the acceptability of winding down or checking out with alcohol.

To a well-adjusted child, this may not have led to addiction. But to a child with ADHD and the attendant self-esteem issues, it was an invitation to the land of substance abuse.

So now there was a mixture of guilt and hope brewing in me. I was feeling responsible for all the mistakes I'd made, but I was seeing how the tools and techniques I was learning to use could be helpful in healing his addiction and my codependency.

I knew that Cameron's addiction was his way of checking out of a life that felt too difficult for him. He'd had years of trouble and failures and a very low self-esteem that he masked with bravado and bluster. He blamed his addiction on the early years of Ritalin, saying that had set him up for addiction in later life. Crystal meth is a powerful stimulant and that's exactly the kind of drug that's prescribed for ADHD. Stimulants create a sense of focus and control that's lacking in the ADHD brain. Of course Ritalin is prescribed in a manageable dose and street drugs are not. It seemed ironic to me that having refused to use Ritalin or other prescriptions for ADHD during his teenage years, he was now self-medicating with a much more dangerous drug.

I wanted so much to share the ideas I was learning with Cameron so that he could learn to heal and take care of himself. My hope was that once I got through the training, I could do some work with him and help him to take control of his own life. I began to realize that every time I stepped in and bailed him out of something or made a decision for him, I was disempowering him. I didn't want to do that anymore.

In November, I had an emotionally charged dream that would stay with me for a long time.

> **November 21, 2003 — Kissing a Young Man Goodbye**
>
>
>
> *I am kissing a young man goodbye. I have felt very passionately about this young man for a long, long time. For some reason, I just know that now I must say goodbye. I kiss him and, with one word between each kiss, I say: I—will—love—you—forever—and ever—and ever.*
>
> *I am very sad, but I know it must be so. I am letting him go.*

The dream was heartbreaking and felt very real. I woke up in tears with a well of sadness in my heart and soul. I immediately recognized that this was about learning to let Cameron go, but looking back I also believe it was a soul-to-soul connection and a true opportunity to say "goodbye" and "I love you" before he died. It seems likely to me that Cameron's soul-self had already made a decision to leave and that we had an opportunity to discuss it in the dreamspace.

The Deep Water Leaf Society

I was ready to let him go in the sense of breaking our codependent bond, but the Universe would be asking much more of me.

House of Sand

Cameron had ultimately (and wisely) decided to accept the plea agreement and on November 25, 2003 he had his sentencing hearing. The judge elected to defer the 90 days jail time just as the public defender had hoped. All Cameron had to do now was to follow the rules of probation and pay his fines. It was a chance to start over. It was truly something to be grateful for just days before Thanksgiving. I was guardedly optimistic about his future and determined to step back and let him make his own decisions and find his own way.

I knew it was going to be a hard road for him. Since his arrest he'd been struggling. He had formidable demons to battle: ADHD, addiction and a giant chip on his shoulder. His arrest and sentencing had added a new stigma: convicted felon. He needed to get a decent job in order to pay his fines and restitution. Non-payment would be a violation of probationary terms. With a criminal record, no phone and a sketchy work history, no one wanted to take a chance on hiring him. He was too proud and stubborn to work for his dad. He was working odd jobs and day labor, but he was going to have to get his priorities straight and pray for a big break if he wanted to put his life back together.

Meanwhile, I was moving along with my CJEA training. I had several books to read and lots of journaling to do to meet the requirements of the program. The journaling was proving to be a godsend in sorting out my feelings about Cameron and our relationship.

An exercise called "A Very Important Person," from Dr. Capacchione's book, *The Creative Journal*, suggested drawing a picture of how I felt about a very important person in my life.[11]

I drew a picture of Cameron standing on the edge of a cliff while I sadly looked on, having only the power to send him love.

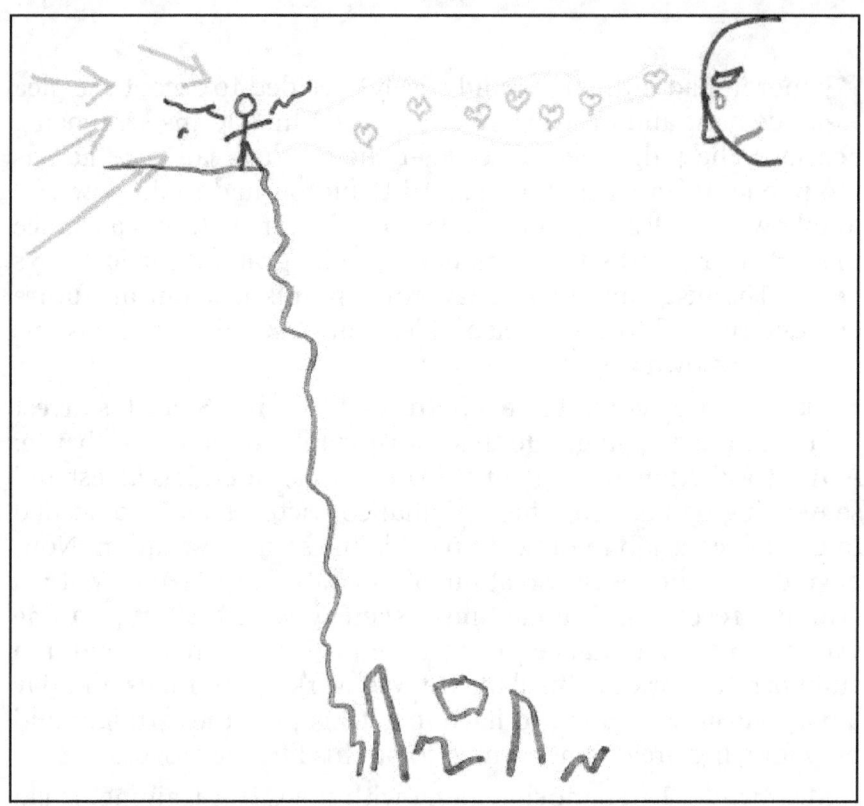

Journaling about what I had drawn I wrote:

> *Cameron stands on the edge of a cliff. Jagged rocks await below. He's standing on solid ground for now, but there's an awful lot of "incoming"— arrows, rocks and bullets. He might just be pushed over the edge by all of it. I am in the position of an observer. I see it unfolding. I have no tools. I have a lot of love and also a lot of fear and sadness. I can't control the situation. But I don't want to see him fall and shatter himself on the rocks. I feel helpless. I don't know what I can*

> *do to help him. I'm learning that I can't keep "rescuing"—he needs to take care of himself. But I still feel responsible.*

In the second part of the exercise, the suggestion was to write about how you'd *like* to see that very important person. I wrote about seeing Cameron standing tall, his shoulders strong and square. I saw him working hard, paying his fines, becoming conscientious and responsible, free of drugs. I saw him living in a nice apartment, keeping up with his bills and feeling proud of his accomplishments. It felt good to hold that vision; it kept the fear at bay.

When Christmas arrived, I was happy to play hostess to my extended family. My daughter, Sarah, and her husband, Justin, came home for the holidays bringing along one of their friends. My parents and siblings, along with their children and grandchildren, all came over to celebrate Christmas Eve. Cameron was with us and on what seemed to be his best behavior. It felt to me as if maybe things would turn out all right after all.

It's our Christmas Eve tradition to do a gift exchange in which everyone brings one wrapped gift and we all draw numbers and pick gifts in that order. Each person, after the first, can either choose a still-wrapped gift or steal one of the opened ones from someone who's already taken their turn. If your gift gets swiped, you get to steal from someone else or pick a new gift from the pile.

Cameron never seemed to have any money come Christmastime, and we had all learned not to expect much in the way of gifts from him. But my husband had an idea. We'd bought a box of golf balls for a nephew on my husband's side of the family who'd been living with us but had since disappeared. David told Cameron to wrap them up and put them in the gift exchange. It was a bit of a gag gift, since no one on my side of the family plays golf, but they fit the requirements for the price range so they were fair game.

My niece, Julie, was terribly disappointed when, early in the game, she opened up her nice little package to find it contained golf balls. She kept begging each participant after her to steal them from her. My brother-in-law, Steve, finally took pity on her and took them, thinking maybe he could use them to play fetch with his dog. Those golf balls have been the source of much laughter all the Christmases since.

Sometime during the Christmas Eve celebration, Cameron got Sarah and Justin's friend to drive him somewhere, ostensibly to buy Christmas gifts to put under the tree for Christmas morning. I could just sense that something was off. In the morning, he gave each of us an Arizona Lottery Scratchers ticket for a Christmas gift. None of them were winners.

Later my daughter told me she thought he had actually gone to buy drugs. It left me uneasy. In the next few weeks, there were other glimmers of trouble brewing, but I was determined not to get sucked into his drama any longer.

A few weeks after Christmas, I dreamed another sad and foreboding dream.

January 8, 2004 — Anthill

I am observing: There is a crushed anthill and flames. I don't see any ants, but there is a collapsed hill of sand and I know it is an anthill that has been destroyed. Someone scoops up some of the sand and it trickles through their fingers.

I woke up thinking of Cameron. It wondered if there was a part of me that should be able to step back and just observe, neutrally, the unraveling of his life —a part that could view the crushed anthill without becoming part of the drama. I could step back, alright. It was the neutrality that remained so damned difficult. It was an incredibly painful thing to watch.

The dream reminded me of my powerlessness. I could see Cameron self-destructing, and there was nothing I could do about it. One day I would think he'd turned the corner, and the next day I'd find out some of the things he'd been up to and it would scare me to death. The dream left me feeling so sad and so angry. What kind of warped Power allows this kind of destruction? What kind of God takes joy in crushing an anthill? And why was I required to stand by and watch it happen?

The night after the anthill dream I got a phone call from the woman who had leased Cameron's current apartment to him. She told me there was damage to the carpet, holes in the walls, graffiti all over the place, missing doorknobs, and deadbolts on the bedroom doors. The place was filthy and stank. Neighbors reported people in and out at all hours. The rent had not been paid. She was calling to tell me that the locks had been changed and nobody was getting their stuff until the rent and damages were paid. It was obvious to me that he was back on drugs.

The last time I'd seen Cameron had been weeks before, at Christmas, when for a few brief hours I'd allowed myself to believe that life could be normal, Cameron could change, and we could just be a happy family. The house of sand I had built in my mind, the house in which the fairy tale of happily ever after was possible, was about to slip through my fingers and blow away in the wind.

Captivity

I was so grateful to have the journaling and expressive arts tools to help me process the emotional turmoil I was feeling. As I worked my way through the journaling exercises in my CJEA training, the predominant emotion that kept surfacing was an overwhelming sadness and grief.

It seemed to me that there was a whole generation of "lost" children struggling with drugs and homelessness. There were so many broken children. My generation had played with drugs, but it *had* been a game, an exploration, which most of us had survived without long term ill effects. It seemed that today's drugs were so much more destructive and that addiction was rampant.

I knew that not *every* child had these problems; after all, Sarah and Ryan and their friends did not. But I saw so many of Cameron's friends getting sucked into this vortex of self-destruction.

My heart was breaking for Cameron and for all the kids like him out there. I felt like I was grieving for all the broken children in the world, including the one inside me. I felt angry and helpless about it all.

I drew and journaled about it in an exercise from Dr. Capacchione's book, *The Creative Journal,* called "How Do I Feel Right Now?"[12] Using my non-dominant hand, I drew the picture of how I felt with crayons: a tiny little stick figure floating in a big, turbulent body of water, surrounded by angry red and black lines and a smiling glowing figure looking down from the upper right.

Captivity

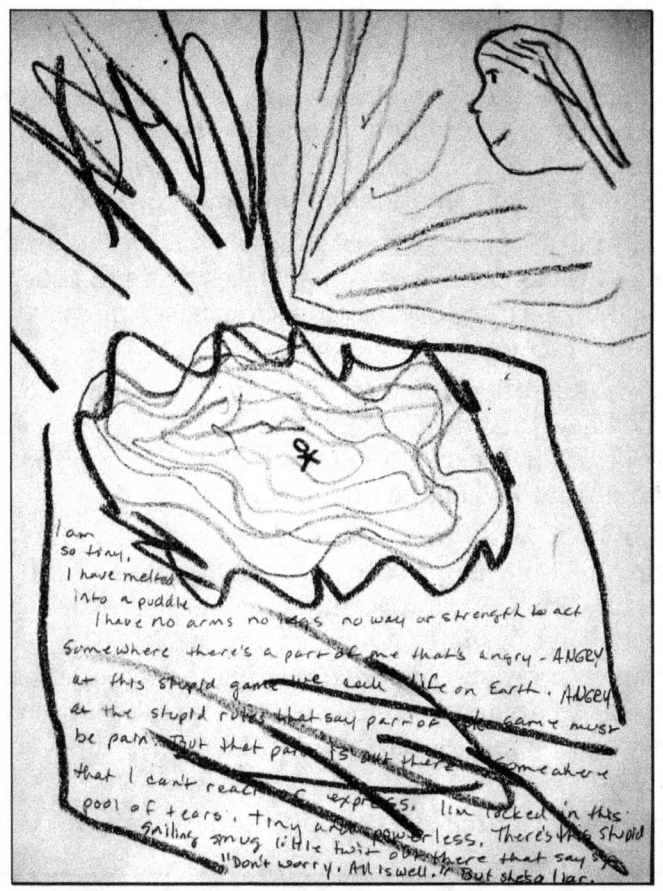

I wrote:

> *I am so tiny. I have melted into a puddle. I have no arms no legs no way or strength to act. Somewhere there's a part of me that's angry— ANGRY at this stupid game we call life on Earth. ANGRY at the stupid rules that say part of the game must be pain. But that part is out there somewhere that I can't reach or express. I'm locked in this pool of tears. Tiny and powerless. There's this stupid smiling smug little twit out there that says, "Don't worry. All is well." But she's a liar.*

Drawing is a powerful bridge to emotions. When it comes to expressing emotions, a picture really is worth a thousand words. By drawing first and journaling second, I could bypass the judge and the critic in my left brain who would try to squelch, deny or explain away what I was feeling. Drawings come straight from the right brain, where emotions are felt and expressed.

The act of drawing is very much like being in the dreamspace while wide awake. Messages can surface from the subconscious and from higher realms of consciousness—messages which words cannot capture and logic wants to ignore.

There was a battle going on inside me. The optimistic spiritual part of me knew that, despite appearances, all was well, all was in divine order. But the helpless, small self was scared, sad and angry about what was happening to my son.

By March, I was gearing up for another CJEA training intensive. This time, along with several other mid-year trainees, I would be assisting Dr. Capacchione as she led a new group of students through their first intensive experience. I was busily keeping up with my assignments, reading the required books and conscientiously doing every journaling exercise outlined within them. It was keeping me sane while Cameron's life spun out of control.

Just before the March intensive, I had the following dream:

March 11, 2004 — Hostage in Iran

I am one of two people who were held hostage in Iran. My identity has not been widely known. I have been asked to speak to a group about my experience and about how to be prepared for this kind of situation. One thing is, you must have some food with you because you may not be fed for days by your captors. I'm wearing a Marine uniform and I walk into a room full of people. They are looking to me for wisdom, but suddenly I can't remember things very clearly. I look through folders and notes, searching for proof that this hostage thing really happened to me.

I woke and dozed many times during this dream, always coming right back into it as I fell back asleep. I had an odd feeling in the hypnagogic, half-awake state that I really had been held captive and it was not just a dream. The Marine uniform reminded me of Cameron, and I reflected that we had both long been held hostage: he to his addiction and I to my fears.

I was finding my freedom and creating an identity beyond the worrying rescuer known as "Cameron's Mom" through the processes I was learning in CJEA. I was finding nourishment there that I never would find as a captive to a codependent relationship. The dream portrayed me as some kind of expert that could now teach people to survive their own captivity. But I didn't feel prepared to do that. I hadn't yet figured out how to survive it myself.

Looking back, I can now see that, like the Deep Water Leaf Society dream, this dream was rehearsing me for a future point in my life. That time is just arriving now. Looking through my folders and notes is the very process I've undertaken in writing this book. I have reviewed more than ten years' worth of journals searching for the story that is still unfolding, looking for patterns and meaning, seeking to make sense of what seems like a senseless loss. The dream speaks of two hostages, but only I am here to tell the tale. Cameron would not survive his own captivity.

A few days later, another dream came:

March 19, 2004 — Confronting the Problem

Cameron is high and I confront him about it. He shows me a packet of drugs (with a funny name I don't recall). I realize from the name that you don't even know what you are taking when you take it—it's like a grab bag. I think this is really stupid, but I don't get anywhere arguing with Cameron about it.

This was something I'd been hesitant to do in waking life—to confront him and tell him how stupid he was being. I had done so in the past, but since his sentencing I had been making a conscious effort to distance myself and resist the urge to step in and advise or admonish him. I think that, at the time, it was important for both of us that I step back. Yet looking back, I wonder if, had I stepped in at this point, I could have made a difference.

I have been learning recently, as I've been reading and studying with author and shamanic dreamer Robert Moss, that prophetic dreams may be dreams not of a *fixed* future, but of a *possible* future, a future we may be able to change.[13] At the time of this dream, I was not really aware of that, and not even aware that the dreams I was having might be visions of the future.

Later, when I learned how he had died, I would look back on this dream and see just how stupid it really was for him to try and get high with an asthma inhaler. Stupid and senseless. And yet, perhaps, it was the only way out of a life contract that was no longer serving Cameron or anyone around him.

The last week of March, I went to the CJEA intensive in California. My roommate was a woman who worked at a prestigious rehab center in Florida. We talked about the possibility of getting Cameron into a program there. I was very excited about this and was anxious to discuss it with Cameron when I got home.

I carried out my assisting duties and made arrangements with Marsha Nelson, Ph.D., Dr. Capacchione's business partner and my CJEA supervisor, to present my own workshop at the end of May. Leading a workshop under supervision was one of the requirements for graduation and certification.

Cameron turned 26 on April 2, 2004, shortly after I returned home from the training intensive. I wondered if this would be the year he got it all together. I gave him a birthday card that talked about making your dreams come true, and how my dreams were all wrapped up in him realizing his own dreams. I spoke to Cameron about the possibility of rehab in Florida. He was interested, but not sure his probationary terms would allow him to participate in a program in another state. He said he would talk to his probation officer about it.

But it was not to be. A few weeks later, he was arrested for probation violation. He had not shown up for his last drug test and he was behind on his fines. He would have to serve 30 days in the county jail for probation violation.

After he was arrested, I was so angry. Angry with Cameron for creating this mess. Angry with the jail for not allowing him to turn himself in. Angry with the police for the way they handled things, making a spectacle of it in the early morning hours in my peaceful neighborhood. Angry with myself for having let Cameron stay overnight. And especially angry with myself for having allowed his life to come to this. I felt drained and defeated. I didn't realize, as I watched Cameron get into the police cruiser, that it would be the last time I'd see him.

I was working my way through Dr. Capacchoine's book, *Recovery of Your Inner Child*, and, as always, the timing was amazingly synchronistic. The day Cameron was arrested, I turned to the book for something to do to take my mind off of what was happening. The next exercise on my agenda was "Counseling Your Child of the Past."[14]

The instructions said to draw a picture of a hurtful memory in your past, tell the story of what happened using your non-dominant hand, and then bring your nurturing, loving, adult self in to counsel and comfort the child of the past.

I drew a picture of my guinea pig, Harry, who had died when I was nine or ten years old. My parents had insisted Harry stay outside in his cage and I had forgotten to give him water. The hot Arizona sun had been too much for him, and I'd felt terribly guilty when I found him dead in his cage.

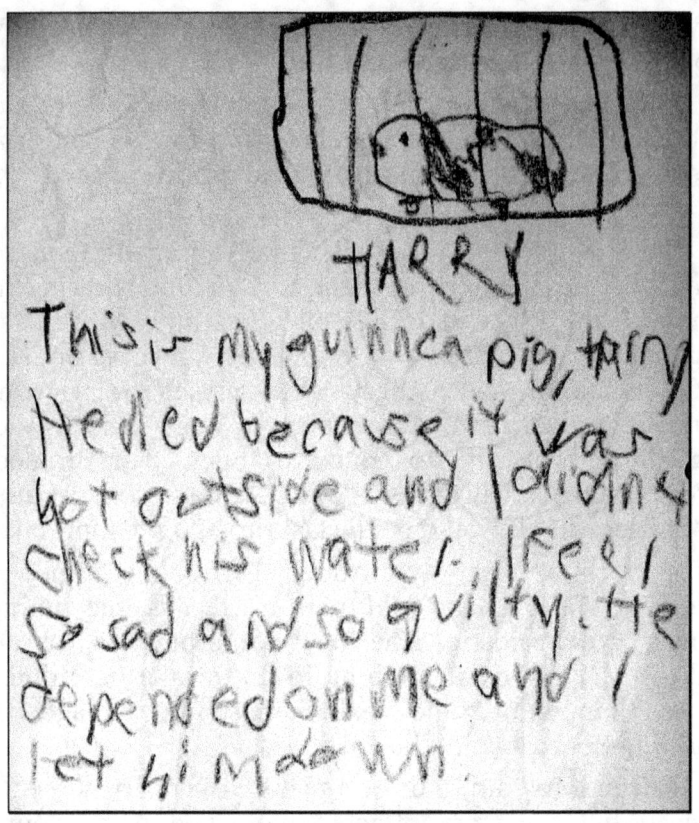

I wrote, with my non-dominant hand:

> *This is my guinea pig, Harry. He died because it was hot outside and I didn't check his water. I feel so sad and so guilty. He depended on me and I let him down.*

Reflecting on my drawing and the feelings it brought up in me, I could see this was very much how I was feeling about Cameron. I felt like I had failed him utterly and had done nothing of value to help him. Harry's cage reminded me of Cameron's jail cell. It's as if something in me knew that, like Harry, Cameron would not leave that cage alive. With my dominant hand, my nurturing self tried to reassure the child of the past:

Oh, poor little one. Don't feel so guilty. You did take good care of Harry most of the time. Guinea pigs and other pets don't always live so long. It is sad to lose a pet, but think of all the love you gave him and all the fun you had when he was alive. You gave him a good home and you were a good companion for him. How can I help you feel better?

The child answered: *Let me cry and hug me.*

The nurturing adult replied: *Ok. You can cry all you want and I'll hold you and rock you and stroke your hair. Can you draw a picture of me comforting you?*

With my non-dominant hand, I drew a picture of self-comfort. This would be exactly what I needed to do in the near future when I experienced the loss that was to come and the overwhelming sense of guilt I would carry for not having been able to prevent it. I would need to allow myself all the space I needed for tears, to reassure myself I had done the best I knew how to do, and to remember I had loved Cameron beyond measure.

Drowning

During Cameron's turbulent teenage years, I'd often reflected on his near drowning at age five. It seemed as though I had pulled him from the lake and saved him from an early death, only to watch him live a life of treading water, ready to drown at any moment.

He kept finding different forms of deep water, drawn somehow by a siren's song into the dangers of drinking, drugs, gangs and violence. I wrote a poem about this in 1995 when Cameron was 17.

Drowning

When he was five, he nearly drowned
Though murky water tried to hide his fetal form
I found him, floating,
Back up like a turtle's shell
Hands clenched tight and body curled
A hiss of air through ice blue lips
I freed him from the water's grasp
But never could uncurl his fists

And always he's been drowning
Like we never left that lake
With friends who are not friends
He's drawn into a different deep

I fear some night I'll find him, floating,
Face up on some city street
Small and lost, his body limp
Blood trickling from ice blue lips
Freed at last from anger's grasp
Rain filling his unfolded fist[15]

Drowning

By that time in my life, I was well aware of the power of thoughts and words to create reality. I had studied Unity and Science of Mind principles and understood the Law of Attraction. This was not the vision I wanted to hold for him, and yet it filled me powerfully and incessantly.

So much of my relationship with Cameron was based on fear. No matter how hard I tried, I was unable to envision a positive future for him. Every day, his actions were creating a deeper and deeper lake in which to drown.

I puzzled over how much power my thoughts might hold over him. I wondered whether my bleak vision could influence his future. I did not want to manifest more pain for him through the creative power of my own fears. Was my expectation of failure based on years of experience? Or were his years of failure based, at least in part, on my expectations? When I wrote that poem, giving voice to all my fears, was I creating his future with my words?

It seems to me this is a question that the New Thought movement doesn't answer adequately. There is a tendency to focus only on the light. We believe we can envision peace and help to create it through our thoughts, that we can impact the lives of those a half a world away by envisioning peace and not feeding the energy of war with our consciousness. But when it comes to envisioning a bleak future for someone else, we are told that our thoughts create only our own individual reality; they do not influence the outcome for someone else. Each of us is on our own path and it is only our own path we can consciously influence for the worse, creating unhappiness and disease in our own lives, but not the lives around us.

My son has his own thoughts and expectations and creates his own reality, I am told. Yet the same advisors also tell me my prayers for peace have an effect in the world. I don't think we can have it both ways. For all the awareness and understanding of consciousness and its effects in our lives that New Thought has brought, it falls short in that it often refuses to look at the dark side of that power.

So, was I creating his future with my words? Or was I seeing a possible or probable future, affected only by Cameron's own consciousness? Was I folding time, stepping forward through it, and actually seeing how it would all end?

I tried to hold a vision of him in the Light. I prayed for him to be whole. I even tried to write a new ending for the Drowning story, one in which he rose triumphantly from the waves, swimming strongly and calling to me, "Look, Mom, I did it!" But mostly I feared a bad end.

Whenever we were apart, I just wanted miracles for him. As soon as we were together, my patience would snap and we'd argue endlessly. My relationship with him became a cycle of fear, guilt and anger. I felt that there was something broken about him, that he was incapable of living a normal, happy, successful life. I felt hopeless to fix whatever was wrong. I felt guilty about that inability and about not being able to harness my thoughts. I was angry with Cameron for the choices he was making and angry with myself for not being up to the task of being his mother. The job of a mother is to protect her child, and I believed I was failing miserably.

They say that fear is the opposite of love, but my love for Cameron was shaped and driven by fear. It was the fierce kind of love that a mother bear has when her cub is threatened by predators. I wanted to protect him from danger, but the danger he faced came from within himself. Unless he was willing to change, I could do nothing for him. The predator was his own shadow.

Five days before Cameron died, while I thought him to be safe and sound, cooling his heels in the county jail, I had a dream that grabbed me and would not let me go. The dream experience settled into my heart, leaving it heavy with foreboding. The dream was a simple vignette, yet it shook me deeply. And it carried a mystery I felt compelled to understand.

> **April 28, 2004 — The Big Wave**
>
>
>
> *I am watching a huge wave break. The water comes all the way up into city streets. In a room, a small boy has peed himself. I think he must have seen or heard the wave crash and been frightened. He is holding a small fish in a baggie of water. There's a tiny eyeball floating in the water, too. I believe it is food for the fish.*

I awoke from this dream knowing it carried a profoundly important message for me. It was an odd sort of dream in that it was very visually oriented, like I was looking at a snapshot of a scene. There was not much action, just a sense of the overwhelming power of the wave and the vulnerability of the little boy. I had a vague notion it might have something to do with Cameron and it left me feeling uneasy.

The dream came to me at the midpoint of my CJEA training year. I had been learning all of Lucia's journaling and therapeutic art techniques, including the process called Visioning® in which one uses collage to create a vision of the future. I was quite taken with the process of collaging from magazine photos, words and phrases. This dream, so visual in nature, seemed a natural fit for collage. I was anxious to dive into my magazine stash and see how the dream story might evolve through the medium of collage.

I began the dream collage early on the following Friday evening, April 30, 2004. I became completely engrossed in the process of selecting images, many of which seemed to be selecting *me*. I was not sure, when I chose them, what they had to do with the dream story or how they would fit in. While most of the collage work I had done to date had been heavy on words and phrases, this one, like the dream, was nearly exclusively image-based.

The Deep Water Leaf Society

I worked on the collage non-stop until about three in the morning when I glued the last of the pictures down. I was intrigued by the result as there was much more to it than there had been in the dream itself. It was as if the collage had grown organically from the seed of the dream. Or perhaps I'd continued dreaming as I created the collage.

Having since studied active dreaming with Robert Moss, I now recognize that I'd stumbled into the practice of dream reentry through a side door. Robert teaches his students to reenter the dreamspace with the aid of shamanic drumming in order to gain further information from the dream.[16] I'd stepped into that same liminal zone in the early morning hours as I allowed myself to slip into an artistic trance through which the dream experience could elaborate its message to me.

Many kinds of water images filled the collage: skyscraper buildings superimposed over images of turbulent waves; dark, stormy, violent waters; placid still water reflecting the setting sun; a huge aquarium filled with fish; a speckled trout drifting in a still green pond. There were also several images of children: a baby being washed in a galvanized tub on some Third World city street; a little girl peering around a Christmas tree, eyes filled with wonder; two little dark-haired, dark-eyed boys vaguely reminiscent of Cameron in his youth. Two women, likely representing aspects of myself, sat at the bottom right as if contemplating or experiencing the scenes above. In the top left corner, there was a surfer riding the waves, and that image puzzled me the most as the action and vitality of it seemed out of place in the otherwise moody and somnolent feeling of the overall piece.

I was anxious to try another of the techniques I was learning in CJEA, a form of journaling dialogue in which I would be able to talk with the collage images and learn their secrets. But it was too late to begin at that middle-of-the-night hour. I went to bed more curious than ever about the message of the dream.

A busy weekend went by. I had no time to attempt the dialogue process. Then came that fateful Monday morning, May 3, 2004, when the jail death detectives came to my door to tell me Cameron was dead.

A few days later Mary, a dear friend of mine who has since joined Cameron on the other side, came by to offer her condolences and a home cooked meal. She noticed the collage, which I'd propped on a bookcase in my home office, and she asked me about it. I told her about the dream and the obsession

I'd had to collage it. I told her that now I could see it had been a premonition, that I had seen the wave that would finally swallow my son.

Mary told me that as she had meditated that morning she had gone looking for Cameron and she had met with him.

She said to him, "Cameron, I'm worried about your mom and dad. This has been a life altering event for them."

He reportedly replied with a grin, in true Cameron style, "Yeah, it's been a bit life altering for me, too!" I knew she'd had a true conversation with him, because that was exactly the kind of thing he'd say, and she didn't know him well enough to know that.

I just chuckled. A smart ass to the very end . . . and beyond!

Every Sparrow that Falls

Sometimes the most profound dream messages reach us in our waking hours. Life sings with metaphor, although we don't always pay attention. The altered state of awareness into which Cameron's death had propelled me allowed me, for a time, to walk through the dreaming with my eyes wide open.

The day after I learned of Cameron's death, a baby bird fell from a nest in my front yard. Already overwhelmed with loss, I couldn't stand the thought of this little bird not getting a chance to live its life. The story of the baby bird became the heart of the eulogy I would write for Cameron.

> *I found a little baby bird under the big eucalyptus tree out front, fallen from a nest dangling high above and out of my reach. Cheech, my cat—the cat we inherited from Cameron when he left to join the Marines—was ready to pounce. It's the nature of cats and I'm sure it's not the first feathered creature that he's stalked. But I wasn't having it. Not today.*
>
> *I put Cheech in the house and I held the little bird in my hands. It was a baby dove, its feathers not completely formed. It was warm and I could feel its little heart beating and hear its tiny little peeps. I didn't know what to do. I tried a few phone numbers for bird rescue listings in the phone book, but no one could take in this little baby dove.*
>
> *I was angry that God would send me this little creature, today of all days. What do you want me to do about this, I asked? Why do you keep giving me stuff that I can't fix? I put the bird back under the tree, mentally releasing it into the hands of God or the whim of fate. I went back into the house and made sure the cats stayed inside. At*

least I could do that. I began to think that maybe there is only so much a person can do, and so you do that much and you give the rest up to whatever higher plan there might be.

When David came home, he found the mama bird sitting snuggled close to the baby under the tree. Hopeful to see that the mama was not ready to abandon the little one, he got a ladder and put the fallen nest back securely in the fork of the tree. He gently put the baby bird back in the nest. Later in the evening, we could see the mama bird back in the nest, loving and caring for her baby. We had done everything we could. The rest was up to the mama dove and God.

Like that little baby dove, Cameron fell from the nest and into danger many times in his life. The world is a pretty wild place and there are lots of cats ready to pounce. One bad decision, one misstep and you can land in pretty precarious waters. So Cameron fell, and David and I kept lifting him back up. And I kept asking God, why do you keep giving me stuff that I can't fix?

There comes a day when the little bird's got to leave the nest. The day will come for that mama dove and it came for us, too. You've got to stop lifting the child back into the nest and let it fly on its own. The world is still wild and dangerous, but you've done all you can do. Now it's up to them.

Cameron lived a precarious life, but then we all do. The choices he made often made his life a bit rougher than most. And the choices piled up until he found himself in a place that was very hard to get out of.

Some of you saw Cameron as a kind of hardass, tattooed, tough guy. It was an image he *cultivated. The more tattoos he accumulated, the more he thought he could mask what he really was—a softy with a big, big heart.*

No, he was no tough guy. I saw him as a lost little boy just trying to find his way in the world. He felt like he was seen as the black sheep of the family, but what I saw was a beautiful little dove with still wet wings that just hadn't quite learned how to fly straight yet. And now he's fallen one more time, and this time he's been scooped up by bigger, stronger hands than ours.

So, maybe God allowed that little bird to fall from the nest on this of all days to show us that he trusted us with Cameron's beautiful life because he knew that we would do all that we could do, that we would love him fiercely, that we would protect him from danger for as long as we could and then let him fly on his own. And I know for sure that he's flying still, straight and free now, relieved of all the burdens he had to bear in this life.

We've done all that we can do, and now it's time to trust in a higher plan in which everything makes sense and everyone is whole and happy. Whatever we couldn't fix, I know that God can. And Cameron is free to soar.

My eulogy was more of a wish than a certainty, but what a lesson there was for me in that little bird's story. Somewhere in the Bible it says that not a sparrow falls without God's knowing it. Every loss is part of a much larger story. Every sparrow that falls has meaning. It is hard to describe how clearly I could feel the perfection and completeness of Cameron's story while simultaneously experiencing the most deeply agonizing grief imaginable.

Robert Moss teaches that the "Big Story" is always stalking us. If we will give up trying to chase our own Big Story, it will find us at the appropriate moment.[17] The little dove was showing me the

Big Story in Cameron's life and death, and Cameron's death was waiting to give me a glimpse into my own Big Story.

There were two things I knew for sure: first that Cameron still existed, and second, that in whatever place and form he existed, my love could still reach him. It was very clear to me, in those early days of grief, that the love between us was all that really mattered. That love was the ultimate gift, the ultimate power and the only thing that needed to survive.

The Music of My Heart

I selected the music for Cameron's visitation and funeral service carefully, choosing songs that echoed my feelings about his life and my loss. For the visitation, I'd compiled about an hour's worth of songs, many of them oldies from my collection, including Simon and Garfunkel's "Bridge Over Troubled Water"[18] and "Oh, Very Young" by Cat Stevens. I'd always loved that Cat Stevens tune about how we only have a short time to dance on this earth. It was wistful and whimsical at the same time, prodding us to live our dreams before they "vanish away like your daddy's best jeans, denim blue fading up to the sky."[19]

The playlist I compiled seemed to capture the mixture of love and sadness appropriate for the event without being stuffy, formal or religious. I knew that Cameron wouldn't have wanted a traditional church service, so I just went with what was in my heart.

For the funeral, I knew exactly which songs I wanted.

Back when I was finishing up my degree, in 2002, I had obsessively listened to Sarah McLachlan's *Mirrorball* album as I stayed up until two and three in the morning writing term papers. I remember Cameron commenting once, as I'd listened to it, that it was a good album. That surprised me as our musical tastes were not really in alignment. His leaned to rap and mine to oldies, new age and soft jazz. Sarah McLachlan doesn't really fit any of those categories, but her voice moves me, and something in her music captured the way I was feeling about life at that time.

Many of the songs on the *Mirrorball* album seemed to resonate with how I felt about Cameron—the pain and the fear all mixed up with love and a longing to make things right somehow. In "Building a Mystery," she sang of a man who was so beautiful and so screwed up at the same time.[20] It was exactly how I felt about Cameron. And in "Hold On," she sang about the impending death of a loved one and how much the inevitable was going to hurt.[21]

When I look at the lyrics of many of the songs on this album now, it seems so much like my precognitive dreams. It was as if something in me knew I was going to lose him and was drawing me to music that echoed my own love, longing and pain.

One tune from that album, "Angel," is a song about the overdose death of a road-touring rock musician, but it could have been written specifically about Cameron. It tells of someone always waiting for another chance to get it right, feeling chased and hounded, and trying to escape all that with drugs only to find he'd escaped right out of life itself.[22] I chose this as the opening music for the funeral service.

Following a brief opening statement, I played "Dante's Prayer," by Loreena McKennitt, a very beautiful song about remembering those we love and finding solace in the endless eternity represented by the ocean.[23] The choice of this song would prove to be very fitting as I would come to find healing and connection with Cameron every time I visited the sea in the years to come.

After the eulogy, I played "Love Is," a duet sung by Vanessa Williams and Brian McKnight, that celebrates the power of love. The lyrics assure us that while love can be heartbreaking it can also set us free and turn our tears into joy by helping us see all of the beauty in our lives.[24]

The closing song I chose was Stevie Wonder's "As." This is an old song from the 70's that I've always loved. Its moving lyrics and gospel flair celebrate the eternal nature of love. Just a week or so before Cameron died I'd heard the song on the radio and was reminded how powerful it was. Interestingly, I wasn't even listening to an oldies station, but the local smooth jazz station. I hadn't heard that song in decades, but after hearing it in the car that day, it stuck in my head and I'd find myself humming it at odd times. Like the dreams that helped to prepare me for losing Cameron, I believe hearing this song, with its chorus of "I'll be loving you always,"[25] just before his death was a gift to remind me that love is something that survives eternally. That was the message I wanted to send to Cameron if he was listening: that I'd love him forever.

Back at home following the funeral, I had a balloon releasing ceremony. There were white helium balloons for everyone present and we each took a Sharpie marker and wrote a message to Cameron on a balloon. I played Celine Dion's "A New Day Has Come"[26] as we let the balloons go and watched them drift up into the bright blue sky. The song was my prayer of hope that a new day had dawned for my son. Rather than death being an ending, I hoped it would be a new beginning for him and a chance to heal all the things he couldn't heal in this lifetime.

Although none of those songs were current hits or regular radio fare, it was amazing how many times I'd hear them playing at odd times and in the oddest places following the funeral. They seemed to come to me whenever I'd been thinking of Cameron. I began to believe that somehow he was communicating with me through them.

The first time I noticed this was just a few days after his funeral. My nephew was getting married in a week. Having just lost my son, it was bittersweet to think about watching this nephew, so close in age to Cameron, walk down the aisle. Plus, I had nothing suitable to wear. The thought of shopping for a dress felt overwhelming.

I went to the mall with little enthusiasm for the task ahead. It's difficult to find things that fit me well, and I expected a long day of frustration. Imagine my surprise to find in the very first store I visited not one, but three dresses that I loved and which fit and flattered my figure. On clearance, no less!

As I was paying for my purchases, I noticed the music that was playing: Cat Stevens' "Oh, Very Young." What are the odds of hearing an old song like that when I'd just played it at the visitation? It felt like Cameron was saying to me, "Mom, you deserve a pretty dress. You deserve all the pretty dresses in the world." My heart was filled with gratitude.

Halfway House

Dreams have been a constant part of my life. For years I'd been recording dreams every morning, but in the first days after Cameron's death, I didn't seem to dream at all.

Perhaps I wasn't sleeping soundly enough or perhaps my mental state was just too fuzzy for dream recall. The first dream I remembered came about a week after his passing, and the intensity of it shocked me.

May 9, 2004 — I'm Sorry

Cameron walks up behind me and says, "Mom?" I turn and I see him. The tone of his voice, the look on his face —it is like he's trying to tell me it was all a mistake, a joke that got out of hand. He's trying to tell me he's so sorry for the pain it's causing me. I yell at him, "No! No! Don't do this to me." I touch his hand and it's cold. I turn my back on him and send him away.

The dream seemed so real, as if I had been awake and it had really happened. I woke and felt immediately sorry for yelling at Cameron and sending him away. Now that I was awake, it seemed that rather than trying to tell me it was all a joke, he was telling me it was all true, and that's what he was sorry for. I knew it was a real communication. I knew that Cameron had visited me in my dream. I wished I hadn't gotten angry, so that I could have hugged him and told him I loved him one more time. I wished the dream had lasted longer and that I hadn't awoken from it.

This pattern of flash-point anger had been such a part of our relationship, and here I was again, severing this fragile thread of communication with my habitual response of judgment and blame and anger. Why couldn't I have just relished the gift of his being there? Why couldn't I have just told him I loved him and forgave him? For the rest of the night, I tried to coax him back into my dreams, but he didn't come.

For the next several weeks, my dreams were sketchy. My sleeping patterns were disrupted by the depth of emotion I was feeling. I had snatches and fragments of dream recall: showing pictures of Cameron to someone, the balloons from Cameron's funeral drifting up into the sky and arranging themselves into a message I couldn't quite decipher, being by the sea and floating on the ocean's healing waves.

Near the end of May, I had another brief dream.

May 23, 2004 — Halfway House

I am thinking about Cameron. Crying, I think. Sad. Then I see him. He's in a halfway house. He tells me he's doing okay. I want to reach out to him, but I can't touch him.

The message of this dream seemed pretty clear to me and the double meaning of "halfway house" was intriguing. Dreams often speak on many levels at once and I wondered if Cameron might be in some liminal zone, halfway between this world and the next, which served as both a place where he could release his addictions and a way station between the worlds. It was comforting to know that he was okay but frustrating and sad that I couldn't touch him. Like the first dream, I believe this was more than "just" a dream. It was a visit, a real connection and communication between my soul and his.

Later I would receive confirmation from Robert Moss' *Dreamer's Book of the Dead* that our deceased loved ones *do* visit us in dreams. There is an intersection between our world and theirs in the dreamspace. The dead visit us for a number of reasons, including their need to forgive and to be forgiven.[27] These visits can be an opportunity for healing and closure both for the deceased and for those left behind.

Although there was an element of frustration in both of these dreams—a feeling that he was just out of my reach—it was nevertheless comforting to know that we could still communicate through dreams if nowhere else. I felt assured that he was still alive in some way, in some realm. I was sure that the end of life as we know it is not the end at all.

Voices from the Big Wave

Between funeral arrangements and a steady stream of visitors, some weeks passed before I got around to dialoguing with the Big Wave collage images.

The process of journaling dialogue with images, as developed by Dr. Capacchione, involves writing with both hands. My dominant hand, the one I normally write with, speaks for my conscious self and asks questions of the images. My non-dominant hand answers the questions, speaking for the image.[28]

It is an amazing process that works because the non-dominant hand has direct access to the right hemisphere of the brain, where intuition, emotion and spiritual connection reside. It was an awkward process at first. Once I got used to it and allowed the non-dominant hand to just write, uncensored by the critical voice or the logic of the left brain, I found that amazing insights would arise. I'd learned the process during my first week of CJEA training the past October, and I'd been practicing it ever since.

I sat down to dialogue with the images in the Big Wave collage toward the end of May, several weeks after Cameron's death. I was wiped out, emotionally and physically. I was searching for answers to that unanswerable question, "Why?" It took me two full days, several days apart, to dialogue with each and every image in the collage. The messages they gave me were profound and brought me much needed peace and healing. A transcript of the dialogues follows. The questions of the dominant hand (DH) are shown in boldface type and the answers of the images, transcribed by my non-dominant hand (NDH), are shown in italics.

The Deep Water Leaf Society

~~~

5/24/04 Dialogue with Baby in the Galvanized Tub

Me (DH): Hello little boy being bathed—who are you?

Baby (NDH): I am what calls out for love, for nurturing. I am content with simple things. I am well loved.

Do you have a name?

My name is Earth Child.

Earth Child, how do you feel?

I am sad for the mother who loves me so but thinks that she hasn't enough to give.

Why do you feel this way?

Because love is all I have ever needed. She cries for me but doesn't see she's given me the greatest gift of all.

But you live in poverty. She doesn't know how she will feed you. Your life expectancy is so short. She bathes you in gutter water. The city is full of disease. She cries for the you that could have been—that <u>should</u> have been. She cries for not knowing how to heal you.

She loves me. That is all. That is enough.

What can I do for you?

Don't become cold. Never give up on the power of love.

What gift or wisdom do you bring me?

I show you the power of your heart.

~~~

The grieving and broken-hearted part of me was angry with the idea that love was enough. How could it be enough when my son's life had been cut so short, when he had faced such difficulty despite my loving him? I argued with the photo in its own terms of gutter water and Third World poverty, but what my heart was really crying out was that in the midst of plenty, in the midst of middle-class, white-bread suburbia, with every opportunity and all the love I could give, my son was still dead at the age of 26. How could love be enough? But the child in the photo insisted that it was and some part of me opened up to receive that message.

~~~

5/24/04 Dialogue with Black & White Image of Boy Getting a Shot

Me (DH): Dear little boy in the black & white, who are you?

Boy (NDH): You want to fix me. But I am who I am.

Do you have a name?

Sorrow

Your name is sorrow?

Yes.

How do you feel?

Sad. Scared. Alone.

Why do you feel so sad, scared and alone?

It is who I am.

Why were you born to me?

To crack open your heart.

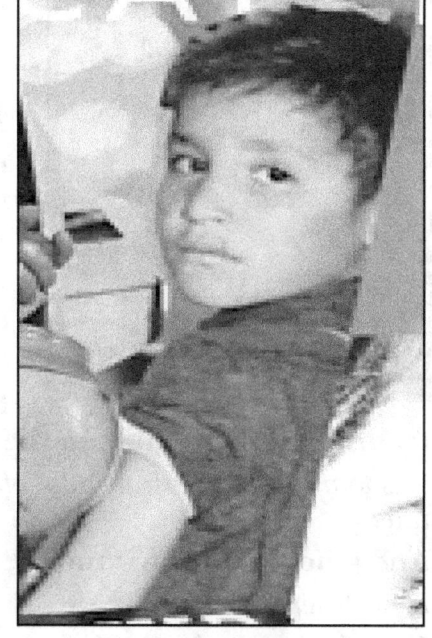

What can I do for you?

Feel me. Don't shut me out. Don't "fix" me —I am not broken.

What gift or wisdom do you bring to me?

The painful side of love is a purifying grace.

~~~

I had spent my entire adult life trying to "fix" Cameron, and through this dialogue I felt he was telling me he'd never been broken. But I was also getting the message that there was

The Deep Water Leaf Society

nothing broken in me, even though I was feeling the deepest sorrow of my life. It seemed to be telling me that these most painful emotions, if I chose to experience rather than fix them, would be the doorway to a more open heart.

~~~

5/24/04 Dialogue with the Boy in Blue

Me (DH): Hello little boy in blue—who are you?

Boy (NDH): I am the Wiz Kid.

Hello, Wiz Kid. What is it you are up to?

Magic. Alchemy. Transformation.

I see. That sounds exciting! How do you feel?

Anticipation.

Anticipation? What is it you expect?

Great things. Growth.

It looks to me like you are feeding the swimmers in the bowl. What is it?

Wisdom in small doses. Only what can be handled at any given time.

And who are the swimmers?

Look. There are three.

Yes, there are three. Is one of them me?

At least one, yes. At least.

Are they all me, then?

All you—all me—all one.

You are very cryptic, mysterious. What can I do for you?

Play the game. Dance, laugh, grow.

What gift or wisdom do you bring to me?

Vision.

72

This dialogue left me puzzled and curious. Through the image of the Wiz Kid and the words he said, I felt connected to the side of Cameron that was always so curious and creative, the side of him that somehow seemed to know more than I did despite all appearances to the contrary. I felt uplifted by the idea that some powerful transformation was just around the corner for me. The three swimmers in the bowl had made me think of the karmic triangle that Cameron, David and I had always seemed to form, so I was surprised that the meaning was deeper and more mysterious than that. The dialogue reminded me that I could keep living and growing and enjoying life, and that this loss could lead to wisdom and vision if I allowed it to.

5/24/04 Dialogue with Broken-Winged Angel

Me (DH): Hello little broken-winged angel. What is your name?

Angel (NDH): Grace.

Hello, Grace, tell me about you.

I am the love that heals all wounds. Even in my own brokenness my light shines through. I am perfect in my imperfection. The imperfection is an illusion. The truth is the glow in my heart.

How do you feel, Grace?

Open and innocent.

Why do you feel that way?

Because it is the truth of me.

What can I do for you?

Accept.

What gift or wisdom do you bring to me?
My own true self. Grace.

~~~

Again, the message was about the healing power of love and the illusion of brokenness. Something about her name, Grace, moved me. I understood grace to mean unlimited blessings without strings attached and with no striving required. Grace was the generosity of God or the Universe, abundant gifts granted out of sheer love and having nothing to do with guilt or innocence or deservingness. It reminded me of the feeling I had after the Padre Pio dream, when Cameron had been granted such a generous plea agreement. Grace was asking me to accept that there was a perfection beyond the appearance of things. She was helping me to reconnect to that part of me that had always known that was true.

~~~

5/24/04 Dialogue with Blond Baby Girl

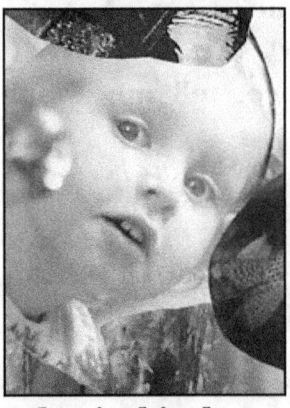

Me (DH): Hello little blond girl peeking out at me. What is your name?

Girl (NDH): Wonder.

Hello, Wonder. How do you feel?

Alive. Happy. Curious. Excited. Inspired.

Why do you feel that way?

Just look and see! It's all around us. It sparkles. It sings. It's magic.

What is this that sparkles and sings with magic?

LIFE! All of it. It's awesome.

What can I do for you?

See through my eyes.

What gift or wisdom do you bring to me?

JOY!

~~~

This little one seemed to be telling me that if I looked at life with the innocence and wonder of a child, I could reclaim joy. She seemed to promise that life could still be worth living and could still be full of joy and wonder despite the loss I had suffered. Although my heart felt shattered and broken, I could feel her promise singing through my veins.

~~~

5/24/04 Dialogue with Surfer

Me (DH): Hello Surfer — who are you?

Surfer (NDH): It's me, Mom. Look at me —I'm riding the wave! It's wild and dangerous and so much fun! Mom, I'm happy. It's all good. I had a short ride but what a rush!

So, you feel good then? Happy? Satisfied?

Mom, I didn't drown. Not like you think. I just grabbed a board and hung on for a wild and crazy ride. Don't cry, Mom—please? That makes me sad.

I'm sorry to cry, but I'll miss you. I didn't think of your life as a lot of fun. I thought you were hurting and in pain.

But it was all part of the ride. Really. It's ok. I'm free. I'm happy. I'm moving on.

What is it that I can do for you?

You've done it all, Mom. Now it's my turn to do for you.

What gift or wisdom do you bring to me?

Freedom. Live your life, Mom. Ride your own wave. I love you.

I love you.

The Deep Water Leaf Society

~~~

While gentle tears had been falling throughout the course of my journaling, when the surfer spoke, the floodgates opened wide. I'm always amazed at the wisdom that comes from the two-handed dialogue process, and yet a part of me always second-guesses the source of the words. "Oh, I'm just making this up," a voice in me says. Or, "Oh, that's just what I want to hear."

Robert Moss has eloquently described, in his book *The Three "Only" Things*, how wrong we are to dismiss these kinds of things as "only" imagination. When we dismiss something as just a dream, just a coincidence or just imagination, we dismiss what may in fact be the most important messages of our lives. Dreams, coincidence and imagination may very well be the most powerful engines of creation and transformation that we have at our disposal.[29]

Whatever the source of the words that were coming to me as I spoke to the images in the dream collage, there was no denying their healing value. But when the surfer said, "It's me, Mom," I was completely shocked. I had not seen that coming.

I could feel Cameron with me, talking to me as clear as day. And, as it always had been in life, my immediate response was to argue with him. I was angry that he was portraying his life and death as some fun adventure while I was so crushed by the loss and had spent so many endless hours in worry and in pain over his life. When I wrote, "So you feel good then?" it was with real bitterness and resentment. I was incredulous to think that it had all been a game to him. And yet it seemed so like him to say something just like that.

But he was telling me he was okay. He was telling me he was happy and that all was well. When he told me my job was over, that I'd done it all, I felt such an overwhelming sense of release. It was both a release from the years of worry and a release from the guilt of thinking I'd failed at my job as his mother. So much freedom in so few words. And freedom was the gift he said he had for me. It was the gift I had felt wrapped within the tragedy the very moment I learned of his death. Whatever we might have agreed to in the time before time, he was letting me off the hook now. He was bowing out.

When he said, "I love you," I felt such longing to be able to hug him once again, such emptiness and fullness all at once. My hand shook and my heart ached as I replied in kind, "I love you."

I was crying so hard at this point that I had to stop for a while. I had wanted to speak to every image in the collage, but this last conversation had left me limp and emotionally drained. When I had collected myself, I turned to the little boy sitting in front of a vast aquarium, but I didn't have the energy for a full-blown conversation. I asked him only two questions.

~~~

5/24/04 Dialogue with Boy by the Aquarium

Me (DH): Little boy watching the fishes —tell me what you see.

Boy (NDH): This is how it is deep down below the wild waves above. Deep beneath all the tumultuous drama lies a tranquil beauty. Look how the light shines! Look at all the creatures—each perfectly expressed, immersed in the flow and tides of life. It's beautiful. It's perfect.

What gift or wisdom do you bring to me?

Come sit with me a while in this stillness. Fill your heart with it. Come here often and stay long. Know the truth of it.

~~~

How I longed for that stillness to fill me. The emotional turmoil of my dialogue with the surfer still weighed on me and I was exhausted. I decided the remaining dialogues would have to wait for another time. I let several days go by before I resumed the dialogue work, beginning with the speckled trout.

~~~

5/28/04 Dialogue with the Trout

Me (DH): Hello fish. Who are you?

Fish (NDH): The self.

Do you mean me—my Self?

Yes.

How do you feel?

Hungry.

What are you hungry for?

Answers. Truth. Vision. Clarity. Reasons. Explanations.

Why do you feel this way?

I do not know. It just is.

What can I do for you?

Feed me.

It looks like you are ready to eat an eye. Why?

To swallow the "I" leads to Vision. All the answers are found then.

~~~

This Zen-like response seemed to be saying that all the seeking of the hungry ego self would finally be satisfied only when the ego itself was sacrificed, swallowed and absorbed into . . . what? What would be left if the ego was gone? I resonated with the need for answers, reasons and explanations. I wanted to know what Cameron's life and death had meant. I wanted to know why life had to be so hard. I wanted to know whether our mutual suffering had accomplished anything or meant anything at all. I was not at all sure I was ready or willing to "swallow the I," or even how that could be done.

5/28/04 Dialogue with the Reflection in the Water

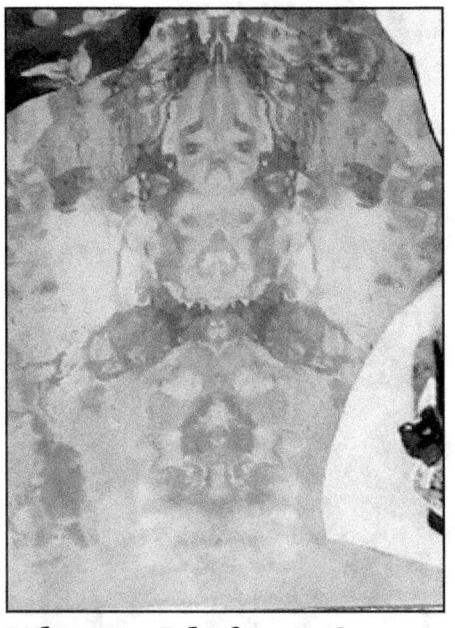

Me (DH): Who are you, this odd, watery reflection?

Watery Reflection (NDH): I am all the feelings and all the characters in the play.

Tell me about you.

My heart is turned upside down, but it still beats. I have breasts like a woman, a penis like a man. I sit, composed, like the Buddha in meditation. My face looks sad. I am human but also alien. My third eye is open wide. I float. I observe. I do not become entangled.

What can I do for you?
Be still.
What gift or wisdom do you bring to me?
Compassion. Peace.

~~~

All the characters in the play. It seemed to be speaking of the totality of existence: all the forms of life, all the experiences, all the emotions played out on the stage of life. It put me in mind of reincarnation and the idea that we come back time and time again, playing different roles each time: male and female, rich and poor, cruel and kind. What forms might I, myself, have taken over lifetimes of experience? Was there a part of me, on some plane of existence, who, like the odd, watery Buddha, could watch it all unfold without becoming entangled?

The Deep Water Leaf Society

~~~

5/28/04 Dialogue with the Buildings

Me (DH): Buildings, I would like to speak with you. Tell me — who or what are you?

Buildings (NDH): The structures of your life.

And how do you feel?

We stand strong against the crashing sea. We will not crumble. We will not fall.

What are these structures, then?

Faith. Family. Integrity.

What can I do for you?

Take shelter in our strength.

What gift or wisdom do you bring to me?

All is well. Nothing is lost.

~~~

The message was one of strength and integrity, of standing tall in the face of whatever the sea might throw at me. And what was that sea, exactly? The loss of Cameron, surely, but what else might it represent? There were so many water images in the collage, each with a different quality. I wanted to know what that meant.

5/28/04 Dialogue with the Sea

Me (DH): I wish now to speak to the sea. Who are you?

Sea (NDH): Life itself. I come in many forms, many moods. The dark and crashing seas and the still, calm waters. The tide that rises and falls. The foam on the beach, sparkling in the sun and the blackest, coldest depths. I am sinuous, shape-shifting life.

How do you feel?

Powerful. Alive. Flowing. Restless.

Why do you feel that way?

There is always more to be.

What can I do for you?

Whatever you choose.

What gift or wisdom do you bring to me?

Experience.

~~~

The feeling that I got from this was that every possible form of experience was perfect and that I could make no wrong choices. I *had* made no wrong choices. There were no 'bad' experiences, just experience itself. It seemed to me that Life was affording me the opportunity to experience it however I chose, and that whatever I chose to experience would be a gift back to Life itself. Death was an inevitable part of the experience of life, and as an experience it could still be a gift. My experiences would range from the tranquil to the turbulent, and all of that was part of the magic and perfection of Life.

There were only two images left to speak with: the two women at the bottom right of the collage. I'd been saving them for last because I knew they represented aspects of me. They were the ones experiencing the story represented by the collage and by the original dream. They were also the ones within me who were experiencing the grief and trauma of Cameron's death.

~~~

5/28/04 Dialogue with the Sleeping Woman

Me (DH): Sleeping woman —who are you?

Woman (NDH): The Dreamer.

And how do you feel?

I will be crushed by this dream. The weight is too much. Please let me wake.

Why do you feel this way?

All of the oceans could not hold my tears. We will drown in them.

How can I help you?

Wake me up.

But it's not a dream.

Then hold me.

I will hold you and you will cry—and we will cry together. The tears will heal us. We will not drown.

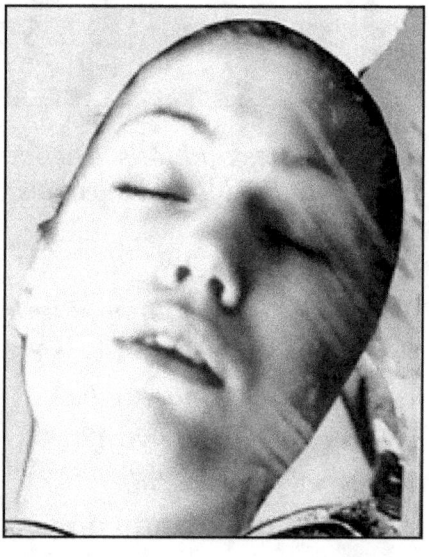

~~~

Again the overwhelming sense of loss rushed through me and I began to cry uncontrollably. All sense of the rightness of every experience that I'd felt from the previous dialogue was washed away by a flood of grief and sorrow. This woman, The Dreamer, was the part of me whose heart was broken, the part of me that would give anything to have it all be a dream from which I could wake. Still, the conscious self who was speaking through my dominant hand was aware that my tears would be healing, that I would get through this, and that I would not drown.

~~~

5/18/04 Dialogue with Open Eyed Woman

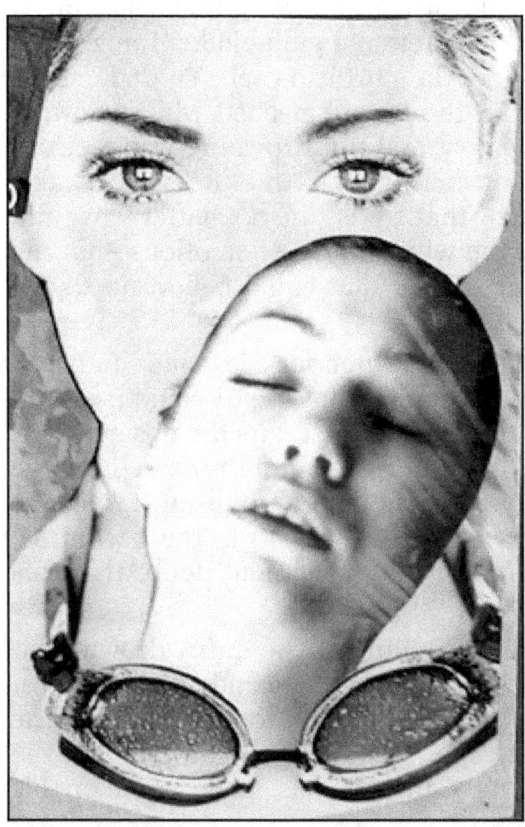

Me (DH): And so, finally, to you—the woman with her eyes wide open. Who are you?

Woman (NDH): I am you.

And how do you feel?

So many things. Joy one moment and sorrow the next. But look at me — I'm dressed for swimming. We will keep our eyes wide open even when we are immersed in the sea. It will never overwhelm us. We are safe.

And what can I do for you?

You are doing it. Living. Loving. Feeling. Growing. This is why we are here.

I know this is true. What gift or wisdom do you bring to me?

We shall see, Claire. We shall see . . .

~~~

The journaling was extremely cathartic. My emotional state had gone up and down, but overall I felt that the words were a healing balm coming from somewhere beyond me. I felt supported and uplifted by the presence of Spirit. The dialogues promised healing and a deeper reality beyond the seeming finality of death.

The dialogue with the weeping dreamer echoed the drawing and journaling I'd done about the death of my guinea pig, Harry, when I was ten years old: the bereft and guilt-ridden Inner Child calling out to be comforted by the nurturing self. To understand that I could allow myself all the tears I needed while knowing those tears would bring healing and not drowning was a gift of awareness from the earlier journaling. And the wide-awake, aware self, the one who knew that I was safe no matter what and that life was about feeling the whole range of emotions—put me back in touch with the part of me that could believe in divine order even in this bleakest moment.

While the first three little boys I interviewed seemed to speak for aspects of Cameron (the one for whom I felt I could never do enough, the one I was always trying to "fix," and the mischievous, magical boy he could be), I had not been at all prepared for the surfer to speak to me so clearly as Cameron himself. I *knew* as the words flowed out of my left hand that he was there with me, speaking to me from the heart. I knew without doubt that this was no trick of the mind.

What a gift that was. He was telling me he *didn't* drown, that all was well. He was inviting me to let him go and to live my own life, without all the drama he'd brought to it for 26 years. And he was promising he'd be with me. Years later, I can still feel the magic of that moment. And Cameron has made good on his promise.

Options

Not long after the dialogues with The Big Wave, another powerful dream graced my sleep. While this one didn't seem so much like a visitation from Cameron, it was clearly a message to me about his life, his death and his options. The theme of water and drowning repeated the water imagery from The Big Wave and resonated with my metaphor of drowning as the theme of Cameron's life. Like the many-faceted forms of the sea from my earlier collage, the dream wanted to show me there were different ways to look at what had happened, different experiences to be found in the ebb and flow of the river of life.

June 9, 2004 — Two Options

I find Cameron drowned in the river. His skin is an icy white and he is cold and stiff. We have a funeral and we have his body cremated. I am sobbing and sobbing over the loss of him.

Later I find Cameron floating in a different part of the river. He opens an eye and moves a little. He's not dead! I holler for someone to come help me pull him out. He's alive! But then whose body did we burn, I wonder?

After his rescue, things are not good for Cameron —people are after him, he's in all kinds of trouble. He runs away to live with some homeless people under a bridge. I am angry at God. Why did you bring him back only to give him this kind of a life?

I woke from this dream understanding there are clearly things worse than death. I wouldn't want to see Cameron continue to live the kind of life he was living before he died. It seemed the dream was showing me the options and helping me to see he was in a better place. The dream seemed to say that in some way, my prayers for his wholeness had been answered with his death. But why were the only two choices death or a living death? Where was the choice where he was alive, whole and happy, married, a dad, all of that? It made me angry to think that Cameron had only two options. Perhaps they were just the only two I could see, or the only two Cameron himself could see. Maybe he chose to exit his contract early because he could see no other way out.

I've sometimes wondered whether Cameron had initially planned to leave this life that day he nearly drowned when he was only five. Perhaps that had been his original contract, but he'd seen how unprepared I was to deal with his leaving. I wonder if he took pity on me that day and granted me twenty-one more years to develop the strength and gather the tools I would need to survive the loss. Those years had grown increasingly difficult for him and maybe he just couldn't do it anymore. Or maybe he could see that I was ready now to honor the contract we'd made together in some other space and time.

It may be that the Universe is a bit like the river in my dream, with different stories playing out in different parts of the stream. Some of the new theories in science propose there are many universes in which every possibility in the soup of quantum potential is played out. It could be that every time we turn right instead of left, a new universe branches out. Maybe the dream only showed me two of an infinite number of possible universes: the one in which I was living, with Cameron gone, and another in which his life had continued along the trajectory of addiction and homelessness. Maybe there were many more universes, including the one in which he'd died at age five. And maybe in one of those he was living a long, happy life and enjoying his children and grandchildren. I hoped it was so.

Instead of second guessing Cameron's choices and looking back on things that couldn't be undone, my dreams began to challenge me to look at my own choices, my own options, and to choose wisely from here on out.

A pair of these dreams came on the same night, a few months after the river dream.

Options

I'd been worrying ever since Cameron's death that maybe I should have asked more questions about what happened in the jail that night. Maybe I should have sued the county for wrongful death. Even though it seemed Cameron had succumbed to his own addiction, that asthma inhaler should not have been available to him inside the jail. Was that what really happened, or was it just the story we were told? There had been several stories on the news about wrongful deaths in Sheriff Joe's jails. I was opposed to suing on principle. Profiting from Cameron's death felt wrong. Yet, was I letting him down by just letting it go?

The first dream addressed this concern.

August 22, 2004 — To Sue or Not to Sue, That Is the Question

I am at a party or gathering of some kind. It seems I am the guest of honor. Old coworkers are treating me to a meal. At the end of the gathering, a woman and man are asking me what I will do. They mean about Cameron. I say, "Well, the only person there is to sue is Sheriff Joe Arpaio—and I'm not going to sue Joe Arpaio. The woman understands. I look at her and say, "Everyone would think I was trying to profit from his death." But the man seems in favor of my suing Arpaio. He speaks to me (I don't remember his words)—seems to encourage me to get satisfaction, to get my due.

I half woke and tried to identify the man in the dream. *My old boss*, I thought. *Yes—Tom Ridge, my old boss.*

Thinking about the dream later, I wondered why I would dream of Tom Ridge, then head of Homeland Security, as someone I used to work for. I had never worked for him or anyone remotely like him. I saw the creation of the Homeland Security Department as a knee-jerk reaction to 9/11 that had only managed to create more bureaucracy rather than ensure our security. Maybe Tom Ridge represented an old me. Maybe he represented the one in me who used to be in charge of keeping my own "homeland" safe and secure. Was the idea of additional investigation and a possible lawsuit just leftover hyper-vigilance from years of trying to rescue Cameron from himself? After all, it seemed a bit like closing the barn door after the horse has already run off.

The dream's message became clearer. Tom Ridge is the guy who comes in *after* the tragedy to try and bolster our sense of security. The damage is already done at that point and security is an illusion. Suing would serve no purpose that I could see, other than to perpetuate my need to point the finger of blame at someone besides myself or Cameron himself, and to keep my anger and pain alive longer than necessary. The damage was already done and nothing would bring Cameron back. Like the river dream, this dream was showing me options. The choice was mine to make.

The same night, I had another visitation dream with Cameron.

August 22, 2004 — Arguing over Photos

I am looking at some of my favorite pictures —memories of Cameron. Then I see Cameron in a big house (like a halfway house). He talks to me. He asks if he can have some of those pictures. I'm annoyed. "Why should I—you're the one who's been out of touch," I say. He says I should have called him and stayed in touch. I say, "You're the one who left. I didn't even know where you were. You have my number —YOU keep in touch!"

Once again, my impatience and anger cut our visit short. This childish bickering was so typical of our relationship. Whose fault was it that things fell apart? Whose fault was it that we hadn't been in communication lately? Who cares!

Instead of arguing with him, I might have taken a moment to consider what he was really asking me to give him. I was looking through my favorite memories of him, and he was asking me to share that with him, to let him see himself the way I saw him when I remembered him with love. Maybe he'd be stuck in that halfway house until he could see the good in himself. Instead of giving him that gift, I was arguing with him like a petulant six-year-old.

Both of these dreams came the night before David and I left for a cruise of the Inside Passage in Alaska. We'd booked the trip months before Cameron's death and hadn't taken the trip insurance, so we decided to go, even though our hearts were still heavy.

It was a good trip, but I just kept thinking of all the places Cameron would never get to see. He'd always wanted to move to Alaska for a summer and work on a commercial fishing boat. He'd never have that chance now.

There was a nice little lounge on our small paddlewheel ship, where a couple had been performing music each night. On the final night of the cruise, I was moved to tears when they performed "I Will Remember You," a Sarah McLachlan song I'd listened to so many times on the *Mirrorball* album. Tears ran down my face as she sang about not holding so tightly to the past and to grief that your own life gets away from you.[30] I felt Cameron's presence and his heard his message, "Don't cry Mom, don't let memories of me hold you back. Live your life and enjoy it."

It was the same message he'd given me when I'd dialogued with the Big Wave collage and he'd spoken to me through the surfer. He told me then that his gift to me was freedom and that I should continue to live my life and enjoy it fully. Through the music he was telling me again. Every minute I spent regretting the past was an irretrievable minute of my own life wasted.

Over and over, I seemed to be presented with a choice. It was a choice between love and anger, between love and fear, between pain and joy, between the larger and the smaller self. Would I continue to hold onto all the pain and hurt of the past? Or could I step into my future in a more loving, open way?

Just after we returned home from Alaska, I had another dream that made me wonder about life and death and why we are here—particularly why *I* was here and *Cameron* was gone. It challenged me to look more closely at what getting it right and getting it wrong really mean in this life. I had felt for so long that Cameron had just wasted the gift of his life. Maybe I was wrong.

September 3, 2004 — Graduation

I am at school. I realize that I haven't been to math class all semester. I'm not very interested in going to my other classes. I wonder if it's too late to just drop this semester. I feel like it's a waste of time. What am I doing here, anyway?

Later I see Cameron. He is graduating. I'm proud of him and actually quite surprised because I thought he'd dropped out. But here he is graduating. I congratulate him.

I woke from this dream laughing at my prior self-righteous feeling of having had things all figured out. The dream made me think about the premise that if you are still here on this planet, your work is not over. There is still more to learn. All this time I'd been judging Cameron's life as a failure, but who was still here and who had graduated? Apparently, I still had things to learn.

The dream said I'd been ignoring math class, the place where things add up and every equation has a solution. Was that why I couldn't make sense of Cameron's life and death? I had always been good at math in waking life. Why didn't anything add up anymore?

Maybe I *needed* to skip that kind of class for now. Maybe I needed to stop looking for simple, neat answers to what had happened and why.

I had come to a similar fork in the road before. When I was pursuing my Bachelor of Interdisciplinary Studies degree, I'd begun with focus areas of religious studies and physics with the intention of learning for myself where science and spirituality spoke the same language. I'd struggled through semester after semester of calculus prerequisites only to discover half-way through my first physics course that it was not the right path for me. The answers I was seeking would not be found in the neat, formulaic solutions of math and physics. It wasn't about the numbers for me, but about the *meaning*. I switched my second focus area from physics to philosophy where I could explore the existential questions, which have no fixed answers.

The big question that comes after the loss of a loved one is, "Why?" There are two kinds of answers to that question. There are the cause-and-effect answers, the kind of answers that look for who's at fault and what could have been done to prevent it. Those answers don't hold the real value, though. They look back to things that can't be changed, things that can't be undone. They lead to guilt and blame and retribution. Those are like the math or physics answers, the "one plus one equals two" simple answers. Those are also the victim answers. They leave you disempowered.

The second kind of answers to "Why?" are the ones that look for the meaning in what happened. These answers look forward and empower you to grow from the loss. What was the meaning in Cameron's death for me? What were the lessons to be learned? I wasn't sure yet.

My whole life with Cameron had been one of fear, worry, fixing and control. Maybe it was time I learned to trust, to allow and to let go. Maybe I needed to learn to live from love instead of fear. Maybe it was time to transfer to some more interesting and useful classes.

Black Heart

The CJEA training, with its right brain emphasis, was about as far from a math class as I could get, and my graduation from the program was right around the corner. One of the requirements for graduation was to teach a supervised workshop in order to demonstrate mastery of the techniques. I had originally scheduled mine for the end of May 2004, but when Cameron died early that month, I'd had to cancel it.

The supervised workshop was the last assignment I needed to complete before attending the final intensive and being awarded certification. I rescheduled my workshop for mid-September at Dr. Marsha Nelson's El Rocio Retreat Center in Mission, Texas.[31] There were some others offering workshops during the same week, so I made arrangements to be there for five days. I planned to enjoy the other students' workshops first, deliver mine on Saturday and have all day Sunday to explore the beach at South Padre Island, which I'd never seen, before returning home on Monday.

Stepping into the El Rocio Retreat was like stepping into a magical little hobbit house. Situated in the Rio Grande Valley, just a mile north of the Mexican border, the retreat sits within an 18 acre wooded lot alive with all manner of creatures from bobcats to birds to butterflies. The grounds are filled with quiet sitting spaces where one can soak in the beauty of the surroundings.

The heart of Casa de Luna, the property's main house, is its kitchen and dining area, which has a one-hundred-year-old mesquite tree for its central supporting beam. The house flows organically around this central room. Its rounded walls and sunken rooms seem to grow from the ground upon which it is built. Tiled mosaics grace the walls in the master bedroom and bathroom. A separate little house, Casa de Jardin, sits nestled between garden beds behind the main house.

Black Heart

When I arrived, Marsha was in the midst of supervising a building project. Casa del Sol, a new 2000 square foot meeting space, would soon be ready for future workshops and training sessions. For now, though, we'd be making use of one of the large rooms in the main house for our workshops. The peaceful, natural setting felt like the perfect place to do some deep inner work.

One of the other students led a workshop in which we used clay for emotional expression. Clay is an excellent medium for experiencing and expressing the gamut of emotions: anger in the pounding of it, sensuality in the slick, smooth texture of it, love and nurturing in the shaping of it. With eyes closed and accompanied by appropriate music that moves you through the stages of the creative process, sculpting clay can be a very therapeutic and enlightening process.

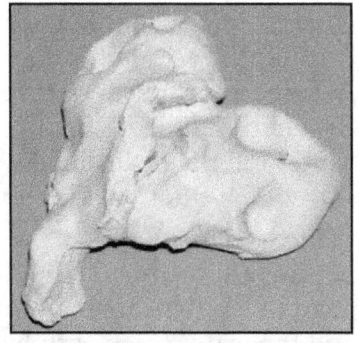

I found myself pounding out my anger and pain, molding the clay into the shape of a heart and then tearing it into a thousand pieces. As the music shifted into a softer vein, I began to lovingly put the pieces back together, mending the clay—a proxy for my own broken heart—as best I could. Opening my eyes, I could see that the finished piece was lumpy and lopsided, with a large crack down the center and lots of holes in it. When I dialogued with the clay heart, it told me it needed time and patience to heal. Studying the piece closely, I realized that the crack in the center of it was shaped like a vaginal opening, and I wondered what might be born from this pain.

I remembered a quote from a greeting card I'd once seen: "Blessed are the cracked, for they shall let in the light." I remembered my journaling dialogue with the Big Wave dream collage. One of the little boys had told me that he was born to me to crack open my heart and that the painful side of love was a doorway to grace. Perhaps there was a reason for all this pain—

some purpose or meaning. Perhaps the light would soon begin to shine through.

The next day, I nervously led my own workshop, called *Dream Play*, in which I blended journaling and expressive arts work with the process of exploring dreams. I used a number of my dreams about Cameron as illustrations for the various techniques I taught. Each participant then used one of their own dreams to practice dancing, drawing and deciphering their dream experience. It was a full-day workshop and quite successful. Everyone felt they had learned much and had a lot of fun.

It should have felt great to know that I'd completed my last training requirement. Instead I found that I was exhausted and emotionally drained. I was glad the next day would give me an opportunity to visit the ocean. I hoped it would soothe my soul.

The sea has always been a place of peace, power and spiritual connection for me. Born and raised in the desert, I suppose part of the allure it holds for me lies in its relative inaccessibility. Desert rat or not, whenever I've had the opportunity to stand at the shore, my feet supported by wet sand and caressed by warm water and my head filled with the scents and sounds of wind and wave, I have felt profoundly at home, protected and safe.

In the morning, I drove to South Padre and I walked on the beach, still feeling drained and missing Cameron, who had been gone only a bit more than four months now. The surf was rough and the water thick with brown sand. The beach was littered with seaweed stirred up and broken loose from recent storms in the gulf. The aftermath of heavy winds and high tides seemed to mirror what I was feeling inside.

I shouted and cried my grief into the sky and the sea. I felt a hollow emptiness, a black hole in the place in my heart that Cameron used to fill. From this place of emptiness and longing, I called out to Cameron. And he answered. Here is what I wrote in my journal that evening.

September 19, 2004. A walk on the beach at South Padre Island.

Dunes, feathery grasses. Gulls, shells. I walk, my mind wandering. Now and then I turn to face the sea—let her soothe my feet and fill my heart. Such peace in the sound of the surf. I close my eyes and raise my face to the sky, arms outstretched. Breathe deep. Fill me, fill me—that's my aching prayer. I think of you, my darling child and wonder if you are around. I see a white balloon, torn and empty, amidst the scattered shells. It reminds me of when we let the balloons go after the service for you. Of course, this couldn't be one of those balloons. But I have to look—is there a message written on it? No. Silly. Disappointment. But then I wonder: Could it still be a message to me from you? "I'm here Mom, I love you." I hope so! I wish it so bad. I think of the work we did this weekend and the clay heart I made then tore apart then pieced together again—a lumpy excuse for its former self.

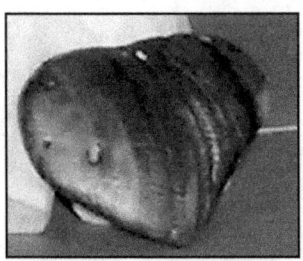

Then I find a piece of shell—black with silver streaks—shaped like a heart and washed smooth by the sea. From you, love? Perhaps. I face the sea and my heart cries out—do you still know me? Are we still connected?

Oh, my black sheep baby, I pray that we are. This black shell heart will always remind me of you. I turn to go back, turn my back to the sea, and it occurs to me that the most beautiful bits of shell—smooth and polished—only become so after being battered and beaten relentlessly by the flow of the sea. Battered. Broken. Beautiful.

Perhaps there is hope for me, then.

The gift of the little black heart brought me some peace. The black hole in my own heart seemed to shrink just a little that day. Whether it was Cameron or the sea or the Universe that answered my cry, someone was trying to tell me that love endures.

On the drive back from the beach, I saw a sign at the county line that I hadn't noticed on the way in. I was startled to see that South Padre Island is in Cameron County. How fitting. The sign was an exclamation mark at the end of an extraordinary experience.

Pollyanna Rising

In October of 2004, my CJEA year came to a close after one final week of training. The second intensive week followed the exact same format as the first. The structure and the processes were the same, but I knew that I was not. Cameron's death five months before had changed me profoundly, and the year of journaling and expressive arts had changed me as well. My graduation intensive became a deep exploration of where I was in the journey of grief.

In one exercise during the week, we were asked to collage an uncomfortable feeling. I thought I would collage my loss and sadness, but what emerged was something darker.

The collage divided itself into two opposing sections with a harsh and definitive black border line. On the left, one aspect of myself was locked into a dark box of despair and anger, self-righteously hanging on to a bleak and bitter view of the world. There were images of death and violence, bodies torn and shattered, tangled webs waiting to imprison the unwary. The self on this side of the collage wagged her finger and shouted, "NO! This is the true story. Life is disaster."

And up in the top right corner was a little girl in a magical gown sending out waves of healing light that couldn't quite penetrate the black boundary surrounding all my bitterness.

As I created the collage, I felt nauseated. I did not like this angry woman. Was that who I wanted to be?

I was struck by the similarity to the drawing I'd made just before Cameron died—the one where my sad and angry self floated helplessly in a pool while a "smug, smiling twit" glowed down from the top right corner saying, "Don't worry. All is well." The black lines in that drawing had been almost identical in shape to the black borders of this collage. Again I was being shown the inner battle between hope and helplessness and the barrier my darker self had built to keep out the light.

In my journal, I wrote:

> There are two me's—the one who is sad, angry, pessimistic, cynical—the one who thinks the world is broken and unfair—the <u>victim</u>. The one who won't accept consolation or grace. Glass half empty. And the one who believes all is well, divine order, calm, serene, at peace, blessed by grace and open to it, loving. Glass overflowing. This one is the Inner Child—the magical child. And this one has the <u>real</u> power.
>
> I'm trapped in the consciousness of the negative one—the shadow. Only the shadow is in control. The power of the positive one tries to penetrate the barrier—but it is nearly impossible to get through. The trapped one is emphatic and

desperate to hang onto the beliefs and the barrier.

(DH) Why do I want to hang on to that?

(NDH) Easier.

Easier than what?

Growth.

But how do I let go of it?

Just let go. I'm trying so hard to reach you. I'll do the work. Just let me. Quit fighting me. You're hanging on to your grief like a badge of honor. Let it go. Choose joy.

That sounds right, but feels wrong.

Let go of guilt, too. Let me out. You think you're the trapped one, but your barrier traps me, too. It locks me out. Just let me in, let me surface, let me heal you.

Who are you?

Your better self. Your truer self. Not a projection of the world's bullshit. I'm the truth. The rest is lies and fabrication.

I don't find that helpful at the moment. I hurt —and that's real! I keep thinking I'm moving past it, through it —but it's all just lurking —waiting to surface.

Yes. Your pain is real. And it will be with you for some time. But flowers are also real. And butterflies and birds. And love. Especially love.

I'm afraid of love because love = loss.

There's the barrier again. It's hard to get through it. I want to help you. Trust me. Let the wall down. Let it go.

Why was it so hard to let go of all of this pain and bitterness? How long did I want to wallow in it? The graphic expression of it literally sickened me. And here was this lightness in me trying so hard to surface, trying so hard to bring me back to life. Was I ready to let it come through?

Later we were asked to collage a different emotion, one that felt pleasant or that we wanted more of in our lives. I chuckled as one of the first images I found was a picture of Pollyanna and a caption that said, "Was a chirpy fictional, 11-year-old optimist the first self-help guru? One famous psychiatrist swears by her." She became the central image in my next collage, which I titled *Pollyanna Wins the Day*.

Pollyanna was the embodiment of that lighter self who was trying to heal me, the self who could look on the bright side and help me recover from my losses with easy grace. I consciously relegated the dark, bitter shadow self to a tiny corner of the collage and filled the rest with images of light, love, peace and healing.

This collage was a powerful antidote for the dark feelings the first collage had evoked. Exploring the lighter side of myself and tuning into its healing power left me feeling uplifted and alive. I journaled about the collage with a bright yellow felt pen.

> *I feel bright, alive—powerful. Peaceful and calm. The energy for outer work comes from inner peace. Hopeful. Look at that smile! Joy, giggles. Something bubbles up from deep inside. I feel connected. The time is now —it's in my grasp. I feel capable and sure. I am ready for life's journey. I can handle pain and grief if I live in*
>
> *joy and love.*

Then, with my non-dominant hand, I listed the qualities and feelings that three of the collage images evoked in me.

Pollyanna

Vitality. Life. Sparkle. Joy. Inner Child ready to play, to dream. She shines. Unstoppable. Positive, upbeat, spontaneous, trusting. Ever hopeful, never discouraged.

Red Woman with Heart.
Radiant Love. Offering my heart freely and openly without fear. Surrender. Let go. Give. Glow. Quiet Power.

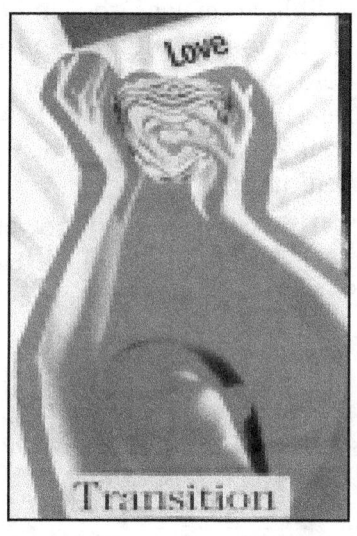

Woman in White Yoga Pose.
Peace. Serenity. Divine connection. Silence. Stillness. Breathe. Go inside—Hush—and be still. Connect to higher power of light and love.

Each of the three images seemed to embody qualities that, if allowed to take root within me, would provide the antidote to the potentially poisonous emotions of the bitter woman in the first collage. I could see that it was a choice. I had the power to decide which of these paths to embrace.

We were then asked to answer the question, "Where does this collage say you are right now?" This is what I wrote, with my non-dominant hand:

> *Time to say farewell to the negative self. Silence the shadow by letting Pollyanna out of her cage. Time to smile and enjoy life. If you spend time in the stillness reconnecting to your spiritual source you'll find it easy to love without fear. The world is good—but people need what you have to offer. You can make it better with your own quiet power. You will find peace (it never left you) and you will bring peace to those around you. Learn to heal yourself and then teach others how to heal themselves. The time is now. Today's the day. Invite joy back into your life. Dance the dance of life.*

I knew that I would still have ups and downs, but it felt like I could never again block out my inner Pollyanna completely. Her light had broken through the black barrier once and for all. It may have been a fragile flame, but I was determined not to let it blow out.

Carved in Stone

About a month after graduation, in November, I had an opportunity to participate in a Level Two CJEA training week in Puerto Vallarta, Mexico. It would allow me to explore the applications of expressive arts a little more deeply in a more relaxed setting. I knew that time spent by the sea, along with the work we would do, would be healing for me.

While in Puerto Vallarta, major feelings of guilt over Cameron's life and death surfaced. The topic of discussion kept turning to addiction and codependency. Dr. Capacchione explained once again how profoundly the family of origin (your birth parents or those who raised you) affects the formation of the inner family (the internal voices that shape and drive your behavior and feelings).

The inner family consists of the Inner Child (who can take many forms from infant to teenager), the Critical Parent, the Protective Parent and the Nurturing Parent. Ideally, the Protective Parent keeps the Inner Child safe and the Nurturing Parent lets the Inner Child feel loved and comforted. The Critical Parent is the voice that says you are not doing things right, you don't do enough, you don't do it well enough, and, in general, *you* are not enough. The voice *can* spur you on to greater achievement, but for most of us the critical voice just makes us feel lousy as it constantly harangues us.

We model our inner parents after our family of origin. If our parents are excessively critical, we learn to be excessively critical of ourselves and the Critical Parent within us gets out of control. If our own parents do not protect or nurture us effectively, we never learn to protect and nurture ourselves. Everyone has an inner critic that tries to run the show, but not everyone has developed the other two inner parents: the Protective Parent and the Nurturing Parent. This inner dynamic is explained fully in Dr. Capacchione's *Recovery of Your Inner Child*.[32]

I began to recognize ways in which my parenting style had contributed to Cameron's dysfunction. My constant criticism and my implication that he was "broken" had contributed greatly to his own sense of self. My expectation of failure became *his* expectation of failure. I *had* nurtured him, but there had been a constant back and forth between nurturing and criticizing that probably left him very confused. My protection of him was sporadic and mostly dysfunctional. I rescued him rather than teaching him to protect himself.

The voices of our birth parents (or those who raised us) get internalized and become our own inner voices by which we measure ourselves. I'd taught Cameron to see himself as flawed and incapable. I imagine that his inner Critical Parent was on overdrive, so he turned to drugs to shut that voice out. His inner Nurturing Parent probably said, "Yeah, that feels better. This is good for you." And his inner Protective Parent was probably asleep, because I'd always been there to bail him out.

I felt I had not done enough to save Cameron, or to teach him to save himself. I felt that I'd failed in my role as a parent. I felt unworthy of the freedom I had to find success and happiness in my life while he would never get that chance—at least not in this lifetime.

Most people will try to talk you out of these kinds of feelings. They'll tell you, "You did the best you could with what you knew at the time" or offer meaningless platitudes. They'll tell you you're being too hard on yourself.

If I'd learned anything from my CJEA training, it was that all feelings are valid, even if their view of reality is skewed. We feel what we feel. There's no going around feelings, only through them. It's important to find ways to work through them, to do something with them. So I wrote an emotional letter to Cameron in my journal, expressing all that I was feeling and telling him how sorry I was for the many ways I felt I'd let him down. It was a good release and I felt lighter for having done it.

After writing the letter, I walked on the beach collecting stones and shells and driftwood. One of the exercises at this training retreat was the art of altar making, and I decided to create an altar on a giant silvered driftwood log that I could tell would be under water at high tide. It would be an altar to letting go. I lined up all the little treasures I'd collected during my walk along the top of the log and offered them to the sea. I thought of the cycles of life and death, of the high and low tides, and of the coming and going of everything. It is natural for things to change and pass away —even the people in our lives. I talked to Cameron and told him how much I missed him, but that I understood he had to go and that I would try to let him go even though I would never stop loving him. I turned from the altar I'd created, willing it to the sea, knowing it would wash away during the night.

As I started to walk away, something caught my eye. It was a gray, egg-shaped stone, just a plain river rock, but it had these two indentations in it that made the shape of a heart, and the indentations were bright red!

I picked it up and looked at it closely. The indentations had the remnants of some algae or moss from the sea, which created the red color. I couldn't believe it! Like that little black shell heart from South Padre, here was another heart gift from the sea in answer to my love and sadness and this one carved permanently in stone.

It seemed an unmistakable sign of love and forgiveness from Cameron. It seemed to be a message about letting go of everything *but* love, about letting go of the guilt and the grief, but remembering that love is eternal and holding on to that. In my willingness to let go, I'd been given a lifeline to hang on to.

After these two experiences of finding hearts at the beach, I felt I had found a place where I could connect and communicate with Cameron. I'd always loved the sea and found a depth of peace and stillness at the shore that I had not found anywhere else. To me it was the most spiritual place on earth. Perhaps it was the vastness of the ocean, or the sound of the surf, or the salty womb water that made me feel connected to a loving and immense Presence as I sat or walked at the water's edge. By the sea, I felt I could talk to God. By the sea, poetry seemed to rise up in me. By the sea, eternity was tangible. By the sea, I felt gratitude and wonder for the awesome gift of life on this earth.

The gentle lapping of the waves on the shore had always been able to wash away every trace of stress within me. Now, it seemed, those same waves were washing up treasures of love for me to find. They were reminders that Cameron and I were still connected. One gentle wave at a time, the sea was beginning to wash away the pain and sadness from my grieving heart.

The Year from Hell

With the single exception of CJEA, 2004 seemed like the year from hell for me and my family. Cameron's death in May had shaken us all to the core, but each of us retreated into our own little world. We never really talked about the loss with each other. My daughter, Sarah, had already been living away from home in another state for several years. After the funeral she returned to her own life. My younger son, Ryan, spent more time at school, at work, and with friends than he did at home. I hoped he was finding support and comfort with his friends. David had his business to run, and he kept his mind and body busy with that. I worried that he might be ignoring his heart and stuffing his emotions rather than allowing himself enough time to process his grief.

In June, my best friend Trish lost her father. Already suffering major upheaval in her marriage, the death of her father, with whom she'd been very close, sent her into deep despair and depression. She had always been my rock and my source of spiritual strength and wisdom. Now *she* needed *me*, but I didn't have much to offer her, other than a shared sense of loss.

In July, my father suffered a small stroke. Another one followed a few months later. While being treated in the hospital, he was given an antibiotic to which he had a terrible reaction. His skin turned red like it had been chemically burned and his legs swelled up like sausages. He spent over a month in a rehab center trying to get his strength back. Now I had two parents needing my care.

It seemed that everywhere I turned, things were falling apart. Somehow, I just kept going and doing whatever needed to be done, even though I was still reeling from my own loss.

David was desperate to see me happy again. He seemed to avoid talking about Cameron as if by doing so he could keep me from being sad. But I needed to talk about it. I needed to tell the story of his death over and over again. I needed to dissect his life and to examine where and how I'd gone wrong. I needed to explore my feelings of guilt and remorse.

I poured myself into the CJEA work and talked and cried my way through my grief with my friends. Thank God I had friends who were wise enough and compassionate enough to just listen and not try to reason me out of my feelings. The anger, guilt and pain had to be exorcised and, for me, talking and journaling were the only ways to do that.

My dear friend Dorine and I had been meeting nearly every Friday for lunch since I'd worked with her years ago. The ritual continued even after Cameron's death. While in the past I'd cried on her shoulder about where Cameron was heading, I now cried about the loss of him and my guilt over it. Dorine had a natural ability to listen without judgment and to offer unconditional love and support. I am ever grateful for all those Friday afternoon hours together.

My CJEA mentor, Barbara, became an amazing friend during my year of training and we have remained close since I graduated. As a Religious Science Practitioner, she was able to offer me support from a spiritual perspective that matched my own frame of mind. Like so many things, her timely appearance in my life cannot be explained away by the coincidence of her having been appointed to mentor me. We were meant to connect and I am grateful that we did.

For years, my twice monthly Dream Group had been a place where I found support and friendship. After Cameron's death my friends and fellow dreamers, Sherry and Mary, were always there for me. Their ability to help me decipher my dreams had been, and continued to be, a true blessing. Joyce, another fellow dreamer, had tried to help Cameron with homeopathic remedies a few years before his death. She was heartbroken to learn of his passing.

Trish (my soul-sister) and I continued to share the amazingly deep and spiritual conversations we'd been having for decades. Now the topic turned to death and the meaning of life and our place and purpose in it. We also began to explore the woundedness of our own Inner Children together. Her losses and mine, coming so close together, forged a new bond between us and our friendship only grew deeper.

My sister Christine and I, having shared the trials and tribulations of marriage and parenthood as well as the new role of parental caretaking, grew closer after Cameron's death. Early on she helped me to express my feelings about the unacceptable and broken state of the county jail system in a letter to Governor Napalitano (with whom she was acquainted from a past working relationship) and Sheriff Arpaio (for whom we shared a less than favorable opinion). While I never received a response from either of them, the act of writing and mailing that letter, which I would not have done without her encouragement, was cathartic. Death is not a subject my sister is comfortable with, but she went beyond the call of sisterhood to be strong and to help me be strong.

And David, dear David. Although talking about our loss was not his style, he did everything in his power to love and support me. He wanted nothing more than to see me happy. A few months after Cameron's death, in an attempt to introduce some lightness into my life, David bought me an ATV. He'd had his own four-wheeler for years that he used on hunting trips and occasionally we'd take it with us when we camped. I found riding it to be a lot of fun, and we'd talked about getting another one so we could go riding together. It was exhilarating and peaceful at the same time to climb on this sturdy little green machine and take it out into nature's back roads.

I loved the day trips we'd take up into Four Peaks and around the Superstition Mountains. The four-wheeler was a tonic of joyful fun for me.

In my journal, shortly after we started riding together, I drew a picture of myself being beaten down by a black cloud of worry, remorse, guilt and pain and another picture of me smiling and trailing a cloud of dust behind me on my quad.

The Year from Hell

I wrote about choices:

> *What do you choose, Clairee-poo, a black cloud full of worries chasing you down, or a brown cloud of road dust chasing all the blues away?*

Something about sitting on that sturdy little vehicle empowered me to choose joy again.

The weekend of Thanksgiving 2004, we decided to go for a ride. We took the ATVs into an area we hadn't explored before. It was a lovely fall day, warm and clear. David parked the truck in a large dirt area just off Highway 60 about half way between Mesa and Superior. There were lots of other vehicles parked around the area. They were probably hikers and other riders like us.

We unloaded the quads, climbed on and started off down the road. I had my helmet on, but David was wearing his hat instead to keep the sun out of his eyes. We'd hardly gotten started when David's cap blew off, the bill of it caught by the wind of his forward motion. He stopped and retrieved it, went a few more yards, and it blew off again. He motioned to me to turn around and head back to the truck, where he swapped his hat for a helmet, having given up on the idea that the hat would stay on his head.

That was the first sign that someone was looking out for us that day.

We rode for several hours and had a really nice time. Midday we stopped and ate the lunch we'd packed. We had seen very few other people on the dirt roads we'd been riding, which was just the way David liked it. After lunch we rode some more and I was just enjoying the day.

Several times as we rode, my thoughts turned to Cameron. He would have enjoyed this so much. It was too bad, I thought, that we hadn't done more of this as a family when the kids were younger. There were moments when I almost felt Cameron was there riding with me. And maybe he was. The thought that he might be put a big smile on my face.

Around three in the afternoon we came to a hill that looked pretty steep to me. It was littered with loose rock, too, and I wasn't sure I could make it to the top. David decided to go up on his quad and see how bad it was. Up he went while I watched and worried. He made it look easy. I shouted up to him, "Should I come up then?" He motioned for me to wait and he got off his ATV and hiked down the hill.

"It's pretty steep and tricky," he said. "Let me take your quad up for you. The other side's not so bad and I think we can go back out that way."

The Year from Hell

So, he got on my four-wheeler and started up the steep incline while I waited at the bottom, planning to climb up behind him once he reached the top. I watched him ride up the hill and get just over the crest of it, when I heard him shout and saw my quad go flying up in the air and come crashing back down. David wasn't on it.

I heard the quad land with a dull thud, but I couldn't see a thing beyond the top of the hill. In a panic, I started to hike up the hill calling out, "Are you okay?"

No answer.

That was the longest hill I've ever climbed. I was not in good physical shape and was easily winded. I would hike up a few yards and stop, huffing and puffing. I kept calling out to David and getting no answer. I began to pray the Prayer for Protection, the Hail Mary and a mantra I'd used years ago about knowing God was always with me (in between swearing and shouting out "Help!" at the top of my lungs!).

"Help!! If anyone can hear me, HELP!"

"*I can't do this again,*" kept rolling through my mind. "*I can't lose someone else. It's too soon. It's too much. Please let him be okay. I can't lose him, too.*"

It seemed to take at least twenty minutes to reach the top of that hill, although it may have been much less than that. When I got close to the top, I could hear David weakly saying, "Stop yelling, there's no one around to hear you." He was alive! Thank God, he was alive.

When I finally reached him, he was sitting with his legs out in front of him and his shoulders hunched over, my four-wheeler laying off to one side. There was a treacherous ravine just feet away from where he and the quad had landed. The left side of his face was a bloody mess where the brake handle of my ATV had torn clear through his cheek.

I told him I saw the quad fly through the air and I thought he'd gone over the edge. He said that the quad flew through the air when he kicked it off of him. It had thrown him over backward and landed on top of him. He was having a hard time catching his breath, and he thought he'd broken some ribs.

I was thanking God he had a helmet on. He'd landed hard on his head with the quad coming down on top of him. Without a helmet, the quad would have smashed his head into that rocky surface and killed him for sure. I felt that Cameron might have been around after all. Maybe it was he, and not the wind, who had repeatedly knocked the cap off of his Dad's head so that he would go back for the helmet.

The relief of finding David alive began to fade as I wondered, *now what?* We hadn't seen anyone on the trails for hours. I had no idea where we were. I shouted, "Help!" as loudly as I could a few more times, looking around helplessly at the deserted terrain. How were we going to get out of here and get the medical attention David needed? It was late afternoon and the sun would be fading soon. How far was it back to the truck? Which *way* was it back to the truck?

I thought about the cell phones we each carried and ran to get the one out of the pack on David's four-wheeler. No signal. I noticed it had a GPS button on it and asked David how it worked. He said he'd never had the GPS service activated.

"Did you bring your other GPS system?" I asked, thinking about the handy little machine I'd bought him to help him mark the prime locations for big bucks when he scouted ahead for deer season.

"Left it in the truck."

It wouldn't do us any good back in the truck.

I started to think of all the things we'd done wrong. Nobody knew where we were or when we planned to be back. I hadn't paid any attention to where we were going; I'd just been following David. I didn't even know what exit we took off the highway when we parked. He knew the way back to the truck, but he was in no condition to try and ride out for the two hours or so it would take to get back. We'd chosen to get more and more remote as we rode, avoiding the more populated areas. And the final mistake was attempting this God-forsaken hill. We should have just turned around and headed back for the truck at the bottom of that hill. Now we were stuck in the middle of nowhere with no one around. David was in terrible pain and bleeding profusely from his face.

"Please, God, send me some help," I prayed. "Cameron, if you can hear me, do something, please!"

I dug my own cell phone out of the crashed quad's pack. Signal! I called 911 and told them what had happened, but I couldn't tell them more than the general area we were in. They had to reroute my call to the Sheriff's Department so a search and rescue helicopter could be sent out. They took my number and told me to wait for a call back.

Just then, I heard the sweetest sound—an approaching engine! I started madly screaming, "Help!" again. A white jeep came up over the hill and I waved my hands frantically. The vehicle stopped and three young men got out.

"Thank God!" I cried. "We haven't seen another vehicle for hours."

"We rolled one of our jeeps down a canyon back that way," one of them explained. "No one was hurt, but we spent the last hour or so packing stuff up out of it when we heard you yelling for help. We would have been long gone if we hadn't had our own accident. We haven't seen anyone else come by this way all day."

What a miracle that they had heard me! Even more amazingly, the driver of the jeep had EMT training and immediately began to assess David's injuries and render what first aid he could. I felt that if they weren't angels themselves, then certainly angels had sent them.

Meanwhile, the Sheriff's Department called back and I tried to describe the general area we were in. Without a GPS location, it would be difficult to find us. The men in the jeep seemed to recognize David's description of where we'd parked, and I passed that information along to the officer as well.

By now the sun was starting its descent. It was decided that one of the men from the jeep would stay with me and help me get the ATVs out, while the other two would get David into the jeep and start the drive out. The Sheriff's Department would send a helicopter and try to follow the road in from the highway, scouting for a white jeep from the air.

I wanted to leave the four-wheelers right where they were and come back for them later. I asked if we couldn't all fit in the jeep. But David was adamant that we not leave the quads behind.

As the jeep pulled away, I felt hopeful for David. But it was agonizing not being with him. We also had a very steep hill to get those quads down before we could start the long ride out. I stood at the top of that hill paralyzed with fear. I'd just seen David nearly kill himself riding up this hill and it seemed even steeper looking down than it had looked from below. The young man that stayed behind with me hadn't ridden an ATV for years, and the incline looked pretty wicked to him as well. God bless him, he just took those quads, one at a time, and *dragged* them down the hill so that neither of us would have to risk the ride down. That took at least thirty or forty minutes, and by then the jeep was long gone. We got on the quads at the bottom of the hill and headed out.

Each time we reached a fork in the road, my companion would ask me which way we'd come in. Sometimes I felt certain about going right or left, but more often I just shook my head. I hadn't been paying attention. He had a general sense of where the main highway would be, but with the shadows lengthening through the trees and canyon walls around us, we soon ended up in terrain that I knew I hadn't seen earlier in the day. Several times we had to backtrack and try another direction as the trail simply ran out or became impassable.

Nothing looked familiar anymore. We were in a wash with huge boulders to navigate over or around. I knew we'd not crossed this coming in. My rescuer was pretty sure it would lead to the main road, but I felt completely lost and scared. I wanted to turn around and backtrack again. We'd stopped for a moment to consider our options.

With darkness settling in, sheer panic was rising in me. I had no idea how David was doing, whether the sheriff's helicopter had found him, whether the rough road out had been too much for him, whether he'd lost too much blood. I was beginning to think we'd never make it out of here before it was just too dark and dangerous to keep trying. It had been a warm day, but it was getting cold now, and we weren't prepared to spend a night out here. My brave and gallant companion didn't even have a sweatshirt or a jacket.

Just as all these panicky thoughts were bubbling through my mind and my belly, we heard engines. Another miracle! It was a caravan of jeeps and other vehicles—a four-wheel-drive club heading out from a day's adventure. We explained our plight and told them about David's accident. Some of their members had passed the jeep carrying David and seen a helicopter trying to land. They assured us that this boulder-strewn wash was indeed the way out, and went around us to guide the way.

While this was definitely not the way David and I had come in, somehow it led out to the same main road we'd started from. In a few short minutes, we got to the place where the white jeep and David were waiting for a rescue helicopter. He was in rough shape. The road out had been brutal. He was in shock and in excruciating pain. One helicopter had found them, but declined to land in the less-than-optimal terrain and growing darkness. They'd sent for another helicopter which was landing just as we arrived on the scene.

By that time, it was after eight o'clock. David had crashed over five hours ago. The search and rescue crew loaded him on the helicopter and took off for the nearest trauma center. My rescuers guided me back to the truck and helped me get the four-wheelers loaded up. I drove home and had a neighbor help me unload the quads. It sounds ridiculous, but David had been so insistent that I not leave the four-wheelers behind, I felt like I would be letting him down if I just left them in the trailer in the driveway. We'd had quads stolen from the driveway before. I couldn't face him at the hospital if I didn't get them in the garage. I knew he would ask me about them.

With that task taken care of, I jumped into my own car and raced to the hospital. I did not take it as a good sign that the first person to greet me was a chaplain, but his news was hopeful. David had lost a lot of blood and had broken about a dozen ribs, some in the front, some in the back. He had severe lacerations on his face that would require plastic surgery to repair. The length of time that elapsed between when the accident occurred and his arrival at the hospital had not helped the situation, but his condition was stable and it looked like the worst was over.

It took many months of healing and physical therapy for David to recover. He still carries a lot of pain from the trauma to his body, especially in his ribs and shoulder. Even so, I know that but for grace and angels, I could have lost him that day.

In retrospect, I know someone must have been watching over us. From the moment David turned back to trade his hat for a helmet, to the amazing appearance of that white jeep coming over the hill when we'd seen no one for hours, to the perfectly timed arrival of the four-wheel-drive club just as I was losing all hope, I can see some protective force in action.

In all the mad panic, I never even got the names of our rescuers. I'm not at all sure I even thanked them properly. Perhaps I'll never know whether they were flesh and blood or had wings hidden beneath their T-shirts.

When I look back on that close call, I can only think that Cameron *was* riding with us that day. I like to think that when things took a turn for the worse, he pulled some strings and called in the troops to bring us safely home.

The Wish

As 2004 was winding down, the last thing I could muster up was an ounce of holiday spirit. With Cameron gone and David still mending from his accident, I didn't even want to put up the Christmas tree. If not for my son, Ryan, who turned 17 that December, our house would have been as dark as Scrooge's pre-visitation heart. Ryan was the one who put up the tree and some lights outside. He was determined that we not let the season go by unacknowledged.

Just before Christmas, one of Cameron's friends came by. The two of them had been friends for years and, unfortunately, had gone down the same path together: drugs, gangs and jail time. He'd stopped by, he said, just to see how David was doing after the accident. Then he started into a long, disjointed and paranoid discourse. I tried to follow his train of thought as he rambled on about the mob and gangs and what goes on in jail. Every other sentence was punctuated with "you know," to which I finally said, "No, I don't know. What is it you're trying to say?"

He wanted me to know that we didn't have the right story on Cameron's death, that he would never have done what they said, that it was a gang killing. I told him the County Coroner confirmed the cause of death as an overdose of albuterol, an asthma medicine. He asked me if we'd done our own independent autopsy and insisted that the County Coroner was just covering up the truth. I didn't want to believe anything he was telling me. It was upsetting me terribly. He went on and on about gang connections, telling me about murders and child molesters and prison riots, piecing together a chain of random thoughts that I couldn't make heads or tails of.

I wanted to dismiss him as crazy, but I'd wondered myself about the asthma inhaler. I had just enough doubt about what they said had happened to let this rambling diatribe start me thinking about it again, wondering if I shouldn't have pressed for more investigation, if I shouldn't have asked more questions.

After about twenty minutes of listening to him, I was in tears. I told him I just couldn't listen to him anymore. I told him Cameron had made his own choices and he'd overdosed in jail.

"Overdosed in county jail?" he queried incredulously, as if I'd have to be dumber than a rock to believe that. "Okay, maybe you aren't ready to hear this right now. I thought you were asking. Maybe it was just me."

"I guess I'm not," I said. "I hope you'll take care of yourself, straighten up and stay out of trouble. I think about you all the time and hope you'll get out of this stuff and not end up like Cameron. But I can't listen to this now, okay. I just can't. I'm sorry, but you have to leave now."

Just after he left, I heard the garage door open. I went to check what was going on. There was no one in the garage. One of the two garage door remotes was in the family room and the other in my purse. I stood and watched in disbelief as the garage door went up and down, up and down, about a quarter of its full height over and over again for about two minutes straight. It was like somebody slamming a door in anger. As suddenly as it had started, it stopped. The only thing I could think of was that it was Cameron—that he was pissed and trying to get my attention. But I wasn't sure whether he was pissed at his friend for making me cry, or pissed at me for not listening.

Later that evening, after drinking a few too many beers and stewing over all my uncertainties, I journaled about it.

> *So—what if Cameron was killed by a gang? Didn't he still cause it himself by his choices? Should I seek retribution—payback—keep the cycle alive? Dear God, Cameron, you <u>know</u> I love you. But, God, I can't go there. Rest in peace. I love you. But I won't seek vengeance. I won't. I'm sorry. I won't. I love you. But I won't.*
>
> *Is your buddy crazy, or am I?*
>
> *How am I supposed to tell now, when you are all burned up, Sweetheart? How am I supposed to tell now? And what if I could tell? Then what? I can't bring you back. You're gone.*

I'm so sorry. I don't know what went wrong. I'm so sorry. I'm so sorry. I can't do anything now—nothing. You're gone. What could I have done even while you were here? You went your own path. I could no more have turned you back than turned back time, stopped the seasons, stopped the world from turning. I ache for the loss of you. I try to bury it—to let it pass. But it's right here, right now. Forever. I let you down. In a million ways, I let you down, I let you down. I'm sorry. I'm still letting you down. I'll always be letting you down.

That first Christmas came and went and it wasn't quite as terrible as I'd thought it would be. I got through the festivities and the family gathering and was surprised that I didn't have the meltdown I expected. I was just floating along, not up or down, just existing. Numb.

Then New Year's Eve snuck up on me, and I fell apart. New Year's Eve is not a holiday we ever really celebrate. David and I are usually in bed by ten. We've always just figured we'd wake up and greet the New Year at a more reasonable hour. For some reason this New Year's Eve, I felt compelled to stay up and watch the ball drop in Times Square on television, announcing 2005, the first year without Cameron in it. I was drinking again and feeling blue. I took out my journal and wrote a letter to Cameron.

Dear Cameron,

Here it is, 11:30 on New Year's Eve. Thirty more minutes in the last year you existed on this planet. Thirty minutes 'til the beginning of 2005 —the first year since 1978 without you in it. I'm drunk—again—still. Not your fault, but worse since you've been gone. Don't know who I am anymore. Dumb, huh? Was always more than your mom—still more than your mom—but what else is worth anything? Why did we come together, Love? What were we doing? Did we finish? Did we accomplish what we agreed to? I *don't get it yet. Me—I'm the one who always had it all figured out! But I don't get this—never did—maybe never will. I love you. God, I hope you know that. I <u>love</u> you.*

Don't know about your buddy. What was that all about, anyway? Was that you after, making the garage door open and close? That was just too weird. Thought it was you—but not sure what you were trying to tell me—that I should listen to your friend and try to do something? Or that he's an ass and you were pissed at him for making me get so upset.

So, been reading James Van Praagh's <u>Healing Grief</u>.[33] Sure would like to have a reading with him—or with John Edward[34] or someone like that. Would you talk to me? God, what I would give for a <u>clear</u> message from you —that you are okay, that you know I love you, that we did what we set out to do and what that was. What <u>did</u> we set out to do?

As I was writing, the New Year's Eve show was playing the top ten tunes of the year. The lyrics, "... *a reason to start over new and the reason is you*," filtered through my ears as I journaled. The words moved me to tears and I felt Cameron was talking to me. I continued to write.

That song on the top 10 just now—and the reason is you—was that you? It makes me cry.

Oh, Cameron. Please—I hope we did what we came to do. I hope I didn't fail you as utterly as I feel I did. Can you communicate with me some way? Some way that I'll hear and know for sure and for real is you? I probably have no right to ask—but I need this—PLEASE—can you get a message to me that I will know is real? Send me a sign I can't miss. Tell me, what did we come here to do together and did we do it? Are we done? Or did I just fuck it up completely and let you down?

The Wish

Were you there with us when Dad crashed? Did you make him go back for his helmet? Did you make those people hear me yelling for help? Did you make him live instead of die for me?

Eleven minutes now 'til the year is gone—worst year of my life but I don't want to let go because I have to let you go all over again with it. I'm sorry. I understand you probably don't want to see me cry and be sad over you —that it probably hurts you. I'm sorry. I'm weak. I just want to know you're okay—we're okay—that we did good. That you know I love you.

Lame this year, Baby—no Dick Clark—Ryan Seacrest doing the Times Square thing. It's just not right. Did you see/hear the tsunami in Sri Lanka just after Christmas? Hope you are helping to welcome those hundred thousand plus souls into heaven. I just don't get this world, kiddo—it's so full of loss and pain. Change— nothing but change—ready or not here it comes.

So, shit. I don't know what I meant to write. I love you. Find peace. Help me find peace. I love you. That's all. I love you.

Four minutes. Goodbye, Love. Goodbye. Here comes a year without you. No more years to come with you—no more you—not in this life— not for me. Peace. Be well.

Love you always,

Mom

After I finished my letter and watched the ball drop, in the early minutes of 2005 I went to the Internet and found the lyrics for the song I'd heard on the show. The tune is called "The Reason" by a band named Hoobastank. One verse and chorus in particular spoke straight to my heart:

The Deep Water Leaf Society

> I'm sorry that I hurt you
> It's something I must live with every day
> And all the pain I put you through
> I wish that I could take it all away
> And be the one who catches all your tears
> That's why I need you to hear
>
> I've found a reason for me
> To change who I used to be
> A reason to start over new
> And the reason is you[35]

Could I dare hope it was a message from Cameron? Could I dare hope that from his new perspective he could see that all I ever held for him was love? Could the power of that love help him to grow and heal and be stronger even now? Is that why we'd come together in this life? Had I helped him after all? Could he make new choices and move forward, become whole? I hoped so. I hoped so. That was all I'd ever wished for him.

Twins

The first few months of 2005 found me moving in slow motion. It seemed that the events of 2004 had knocked the wind out of me, pulled some plug in me through which all my energy and motivation had drained away. I would think about doing lots of things, but never quite get around to doing them. Mostly I slept and read books and watched TV. I had also become very edgy, like a porcupine ready to raise its quills at the slightest provocation. Anyone who came too close was at risk for injury. I craved isolation and solitude like an injured animal wanting to lick my wounds in peace. And all the while, I loathed myself for it.

On St. Patrick's Day, I had to have my dog, Maia, put to sleep. She'd been wasting away for some time, not eating, getting weaker. The veterinarian had run a lot of tests, but had not been able to discover the cause of her problems. She was suffering so much that it finally seemed that the only humane option was to euthanize her.

I felt losses piled upon losses until it seemed I couldn't tell the large from the small anymore. I just felt empty and used up.

Through a book I had read, I found a grief support group on the Internet and started reading the posts there.[36] Soon I began to post my own comments as well. All the people in the group were going through the same kinds of things that I had been experiencing and suddenly I didn't feel so isolated. Some people had experienced a loss very recently, and I could see how far I'd come since those first days of raw pain. Some had come farther than I had in the journey of healing. Each of us did what we could to help the others along. I gained strength by being able to share my story and the tools I'd been using to get through my grief. But it was so hard to hear the others' stories, and often I just didn't know what to say. I was still trying to make sense of this emotional roller coaster called grief.

I continued to draw and to journal. Toward the end of March I drew a portrait of my feelings, and what I drew felt ugly to me.

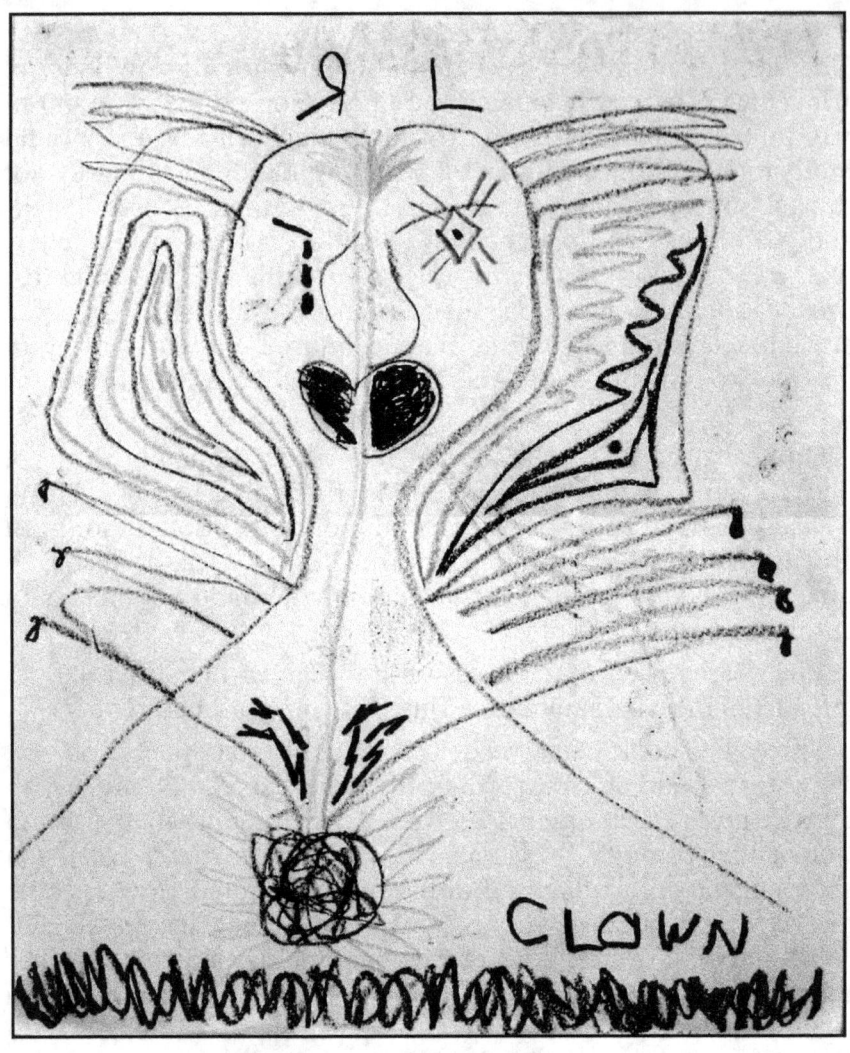

I titled the drawing, "Clown," and wrote:
> *This is not the beautiful kind of image I wanted to draw. It sickens me on many levels. I feel*

contempt for myself—as an artist, as a person, as a being of spiritual light. This is ugly—This is me.

There is sorrow, grief, pain, anger, confusion. My gown—its collar is like a porcupine—I prick, stab, draw blood, cry blood, send jagged bloody spears into my own heart. There is light there still—potential. Connection from heart chakra to third eye, but nothing at the throat and the mouth is full of darkness, blackness, emptiness.

Clown, I call this one. Clown, jokester, jester, fool. All dressed up in this ridiculous costume making like a fool.

I'm ANGRY—this feels so angry. What's wrong with this planet? Why so much pain, loss, helplessness?

(DH) I imagined drawing a lovely picture and out you came instead. Who the hell are you?

(NDH): Yes. Who the HELL. Your very own hell.

What do you want?

To stay with you and torture you forever.

Why?

Why not?

You scare me. I don't like you.

I don't care.

I want you to leave.

HA HA HA.

Why have you come to me?

You opened the door and let me in.

Well now I'm opening the door and kicking you <u>OUT!</u>

HA! You are weak.

What do you want from me?

I feed on your pain.

> **You can have my pain. Take it all. Just take it and <u>Leave</u>.**
>
> *No.*
>
> **How can I make you leave? I believe I can make you leave if I STARVE YOU to death. I have to stop feeding you my pain. Isn't that so?**
>
> *Wailing. Wailing.*
>
> **I will figure out how to stop feeding you and you will cease to exist. I banish you!**
>
> *You are weak and stupid. You will fail.*
>
> **No. I will succeed. Pack your bags. You will be gone very soon.**

~~~

In *The Four Agreements*, Don Miguel Ruiz wrote about the parasite, that false energy that comes to life within the self, but is *not* the self.[37] The parasite thrives on drama and pain. It is born from all the false stories we create about who we are and how we are not enough. Here it was, in my drawing and in this dialogue, rearing its ugly head. The difficulty with the parasite is that it takes on a life of its own and it does not relinquish that life easily. Once you resolve to change, the parasite fights back and hangs on for dear life.

I had recognized, in reading the posts at the grief website, that there were two kinds of people when it came to grief: those that came in from day one, holding their bleeding hearts in their hands, but determined to heal, and those who would cling to their grief for the rest of their lives, resisting healing every step of the way. I don't mean this as a judgment, simply an observation. Now I was observing it in myself. Who was going to win this battle, my true self or the parasite?

Enough was enough. It was time to detach myself from the vampire energy that was feeding on my pain and keeping me in this half-life state. Cameron's birthday was coming up and, a month later, the one-year anniversary of his death. As I considered those two events, I knew that they should mark a turning point in my journey of grief. The traditional one year of mourning would be over. It was time to let go of the past and start living for the future. I planned to release a white balloon with a message to Cameron on each of those days, but I wasn't sure what I wanted to say.

A few days later I sat in my garden journaling out my thoughts about writing a book. For some time I'd had a story idea for a novel and I was beginning to feel that it was time to start writing it. As I journaled, a movement caught my eye. I looked up to see a single white balloon floating by in the bright blue sky above my yard.

I stopped to watch it, determined to watch it until I could no longer see it, taking it as a hello from Cameron. It was moving east, the same direction Cameron's funeral balloons had traveled, but then it got caught in a draft that circled it back around until it was directly overhead. As I gazed upward, it started to travel up and up getting smaller and smaller. A gust of wind rattled the pages of my journal, tearing the drawing of the ugly clown from its pocket and throwing it to the ground. I reached down to pick it up, and when I looked back to the sky, the balloon was out of sight.

It seemed like Cameron was telling me to let go of all that anger, grief and ugliness—to throw it away as the wind had thrown the drawing. I thought I could hear him saying, "Let it go. Let me go. Write your story. It will be a good one." When his birthday came, I wrote in my journal.

> *Today is Cameron's birthday. He would be 27. I want to release a balloon, but it's Saturday and David's home and I feel self-conscious about it. That's silly, I guess—but I'm uncomfortable. I wanted this to be my own private ceremony, just like my grief has been, for the most part, my own private grief. How stupid and sad is that?*
>
> *But Happy Birthday, Cameron. I love you and I hope that wherever you are and whatever form your current existence takes, that you are happy and can see the whole picture and understand*

how it was all good—it is all good—you are all good. You deserve wholeness and happiness and I hope that at last you've found it, allowed yourself to have it. I miss you, but life is good and will continue to be good for me. Thank you for your hellos that I seem to experience now and then. Was that balloon from you on Wednesday? I think it was, and it was very special. So thank you.

You must know about Maia—I hope she's with you. I know how you always need to have a pet to take care of and to love. I miss you, but things are getting better. I don't cry as often. There is still a place in my heart—always will be—that only you can fill. But maybe that place isn't as empty as it felt at first. Maybe you are still filling it and I just thought it was empty. Well, Happy Birthday. Sorry I'm such a chicken shit about sending you a balloon.

I love you.

Mom

The night before the anniversary of Cameron's passing, I went to sleep inviting Cameron to come to me in a dream. In the morning, this is what I remembered.

May 3, 2005 — Twins

The doctor tells me I'm pregnant. Oh my God, I don't want to have another baby at this age—I'm 47 years old! It will be so much work and I don't have the energy. I love babies, but I don't want one of my own. But I'm torn, I can't have an abortion because I feel like God must have given me this baby and I can't turn away from that. I hope that maybe the doctor is wrong. But no, later I learn that not only am I pregnant, I'm having twins.

I was frustrated that I hadn't dreamed about Cameron, but I wondered if there was a message from him in this dream.

I wondered who these twin babies might be. My first thought was they might represent my future work. Perhaps one was the book I wanted to write and the other was my coaching practice. Or maybe they represented the basic dichotomy or polarity of living: good and evil, right and wrong, light and dark. Maybe Cameron was telling me that my life would always include both and that while his death may feel dark, there was a light side too.

My friend Barbara had sent me an email the day before saying she'd "mentally visited" with Cameron and his message to me was that I should put aside my sorrow and live in joy. That had also seemed to be the message when the balloon circled my yard and the ugly clown blew out of my journal. I pondered the meaning of the dream as I went to the party store to buy a single white helium balloon.

Later, I wrote an email to my online friends.

> Today marks one year since my beautiful boy left us. It seems impossible that it's been that long. But, looking back, I must admit that some healing has occurred and the edges of the wound are not quite so exposed and painful. There is still a hole in my heart that only Cameron can fill, but sometimes I'm surprised to find that he **is** filling it even though he's no longer here. Something of him **is** here.
>
> I have been getting messages from him in various ways—at least I believe they are from him. Sometimes in a song on the radio, sometimes in a dream, sometimes in little things I find as I walk and think of him. I have friends who've received messages from him while they meditate or pray. The theme seems always to be: "Let go of all the sorrow, Mom, and live your life in joy—for me." And I'm trying to do that.
>
> Last night I dreamed I was pregnant with twins and I think the twins are joy and sorrow,

and I think I can carry them both and love them both and honor them both. I think that's what life asks us to do.

Today, in memory of Cameron, I let go a single white balloon. With it I let go of just a little more sorrow and, while watching it sail up into the sky, I breathed in a little more joy. That's what he would want from me.

The Medium

In my New Year's Eve ramblings, I had journaled about my wish to have a reading with a medium. *Ghost Whisperer* and *Medium* were two of my favorite TV shows, and I was envious of the characters' abilities to seemingly communicate with the dead in a normal conversation. Not that I'd want to be inundated with the presence of every dead Tom, Dick and Harry out there—I just wanted to be able to talk to Cameron like that.

Even though I'd dreamed of Cameron and he'd spoken to me when I dialogued with The Big Wave collage, and even though I'd often heard songs on the radio that seemed to be messages from him, I was not certain that those experiences were anything more than my imagination or wishful thinking.

Allison DuBois, the real-life medium upon whose life the show *Medium* is based, is a local Phoenix girl. I'd gone so far as to look up her website to see if I could afford a reading with her.[38] I was disappointed to find that because her visibility had increased significantly since the show had become popular, she was no longer able to offer readings to the public. The thought of a private session with a medium was kind of a pipe dream, but it really felt like the only way I might get a clear message from Cameron. I guess he was listening, because it didn't take long for the wheels to be set in motion.

In the first few months of 2005, I began to focus on how I could help people using all the wonderful tools I'd learned in CJEA. I put my intention out to the Universe, and soon the right information and connections started coming my way. I heard an advertisement on the radio for a school called the Southwest Institute of Healing Arts (SWIHA).[39] The school was in Tempe, not far from me, so I decided to check it out. SWIHA offered training and certification in massage therapy, hypnotherapy, yoga, holistic healthcare, life coaching and more. The building itself seemed to hold an amazing energy—its halls lined with artwork and room after room in which healing modalities were constantly being taught. I felt right at home the minute I walked in. In January, I signed up for SWIHA's Transformational Life Coaching training program. Coaching seemed like the perfect way to package what I had to offer. The training would begin in June.

While I was at the school signing up for the coaching program, I picked up a couple of free holistic newspapers thinking they'd be a good place in which to advertise my services. I brought them home and they sat on my messy office desk, other papers accumulating on top of them, as I busied myself with upgrading my web site, mapping out workshops and scouting locations where I could teach.

At some point a few months later, I dug those newspapers out and browsed through them. In one of them I came across an advertisement for a new organization called the Arizona Holistic Chamber of Commerce (AZHCC).[40] I was intrigued with the concept of a Chamber of Commerce focused on holistic businesses and the art of practicing business from a holistic perspective. What a great way to promote my business and network with others who are walking the same path, I thought. I went to the April luncheon and found the other members to be so warm and welcoming that I signed up for membership then and there.

The May meeting was to be an evening mixer, with hors d'oeuvres and a cash bar, during which there would be a silent auction to raise funds for the Chamber. What fun, I thought, as I put the event on my calendar. Little did I know what doors would be opening for me that night.

Many of the items in the silent auction were for services donated by Chamber members. There were spa packages and massages, reiki sessions and coaching packages, feng shui consultations and a myriad of other offerings. When the auction opened for bidding, I wandered around the display tables trying to decide on which one or two items I would bid. I had an amount in mind that I was willing to spend to help get this brand new holistic organization off and running. I looked at every item being offered and finally settled on a feng shui consultation,

The Medium

which might help me clear the clutter in my office, and a massage package, which might help to clear my internal clutter. I put a low bid on each and continued to mingle, checking back at the tables every now and then to see if I'd been outbid.

In my half-dozen rounds of the auction tables, I knew that I had seen every item up for bid. But the last time I went around, a new item caught my eye. I *swear* it had not been there before.

It was a certificate for a one-hour private session with a local medium.

My heart jumped with excitement as I wrote a number on the empty bid sheet. Apparently, no one else had seen it either, and there were only a few minutes left before the auction closed.

I quickly checked the other items I'd been interested in and found I'd been outbid on both. Kismet! I could focus all my resources on the medium's certificate and still stay in my budget. I saw someone else put in a bid on the session and immediately went to outbid them. Just as I wrote my final figure on the sheet, time was called. The auction was over and the medium's session was mine!

I had an eerie feeling that Cameron was pulling strings again. It was just too coincidental that the item had shown up at the last minute and that only one other person had competed with me in the final minutes of bidding. As a matter of fact, in retrospect, the whole chain of events that had brought me to the auction that evening seemed now as if they'd been orchestrated to guide me every step of the way. I couldn't wait to get home and make an appointment with the psychic.

On June 1st, five months to the day from my journaled plea for a clear message from Cameron, I met with the medium, Jamie Clark.[41] I have a strong skeptical streak in me and even though I believed in the validity of psychic communication in theory, I knew there were a lot of charlatans out there. I put on my best poker face and vowed not to give Jamie anything to work with. If Cameron was going to speak to me, I wanted to know for sure that I wasn't leading the conversation with my own words and explanations. Jamie knew nothing about me, we had never even met, and I didn't tell him anything about who I was hoping to contact.

He started out with a brief general reading of my life and health and a description of his work and how he'd come into it. Then he asked me whether I wanted to have a psychic life reading (a look at things that would be coming up for me), or if I wanted to have a medium reading and connect to someone who'd passed.

I told him the latter, a connection to someone who'd passed. I took out a notepad and pencil and asked him if he minded my taking notes. He didn't mind at all. He said that was a good way not to miss anything and that some people even recorded their sessions. I wished I had thought of that. My pencil went non-stop for the next hour as Jamie talked.

He told me there was a mother or mother-in-law presence with a strong cancerous energy. My mother-in-law had died of cancer a few years back. He also was picking up two grandfather figures, one with farmer or gardener energy and one more intellectual. Both my grandfathers were long dead, and I knew that my mother's family had worked a small, Depression-era farm. He seemed to be tuning into things that were true, but I so wanted to hear from Cameron.

"And there's a very strong energy at your side. This usually indicates a sibling or peer. But it could be a child, an adult child. It is male energy, very strong," Jamie said.

My heart skipped a beat—*Cameron! Is it you?* I didn't say a word aloud.

"This is fairly new energy. So, I'm hoping you didn't lose a child, but that's what I'm picking up. Recent loss. He says he's okay. He says he talks to you all the time, but you're not listening."

I couldn't stop the tears that welled up in my eyes. What I'd so longed to know—he says he's okay! *Oh, but I am listening, Cameron. I am.*

"He feels young, like a child, but he's an old soul. Smarter than you. Sorry, that's what comes through."

Now I was sure it was Cameron—he always did think he was smarter than me and, in truth, he probably was!

"He's loving where he is—he gets that it's all energy. He's having a good time. The energy is new. Feels like he passed within the last three years."

So far, this was feeling authentic.

"I'm getting an 'M' name. Mark, Michael? I can't quite get it. Not him, but someone he's with, a friend or companion."

This didn't make any sense to me at the time, but later in the session it would begin to.

"I'm getting 'aach,'" Jamie said, as he held his hands up to his throat. "Cut off air. Maybe drowned or a fire? I hope not. But I'm getting 'air cut off, I'm done.'"

That seemed to fit. If he really did overdose on an asthma medicine, that would affect the airways. It seemed interesting, too, that the word "drowned" came up, given my metaphor of drowning as the theme I'd so often used to describe the course of Cameron's life.

Jamie continued, "He's showing me an impact, like a collision, a crash. I'm getting father energy. Your husband, maybe?"

Oh my God, I thought, *he's talking about David's accident.* I wanted to ask if he was there that day, if he'd helped us the way I thought he might have. But I still didn't want to give anything away or feed ideas to Jamie. I wanted to be able to know this was real. So I continued to say nothing, to acknowledge nothing with even a nod or a gesture. Only my tears betrayed the impact this conversation was having on me.

Jamie began to giggle. "He's so glad you finally came! He's dancing the chicken dance—buck, buck, buck. He's so funny."

I thought that maybe he was teasing me about how scared I'd been the day of the accident. Or maybe he was talking about his birthday, when I'd been too chicken to send up a balloon.

"He says, 'thanks for the memories,' and he's showing me, like a book form, writing, like a book or a journal."

I had recently written in my journal what would later become the opening chapters of this book, the story of Cameron's death and an overview of his life. I wondered then if that's what Cameron might be talking about. I wonder now if, unbound from time and space as we know it, he might have peeked ahead and seen that his story, and mine, would become this book someday.

"Really strong energy. He has a very strong personality, takes over everything, charismatic."

Well, that was the understatement of the century! Cameron's presence had always been larger than life.

"He wants you to take an angel pin," Jamie said, pointing to a small basket on the table. "When they ask that, I have to honor it. He wants you to take one. It's from him."

I carefully sorted through the basket of multicolored angel pins and finally selected a blue one.

"He says, 'Wow, so you can make a decision after all!' He's teasing you. Sometimes you go through all the options and get so bogged down you can't decide on anything."

That was exactly what I'd struggled with since leaving my computer programming career. I'd been chasing one certification after another, like a drunken honeybee flitting from flower to flower, but never landing for long. There were so many paths I might follow, I was afraid to choose just one. I'd left my old career, finished a new degree, earned my CJEA certification and now I was getting ready to take Transformational Life Coaching training. It never seemed to be enough. I never felt educated or credentialed enough to take the next step out into making a career of it. Still, surely everyone struggled with this kind of uncertainty now and then. It could be a shot in the dark, my skeptical self insisted.

"He says he's enjoying dirt bikes and stuff where he is. Shows me riding mountain bikes, off-roading."

Again, I thought of the day on the quads when David had his accident, and I felt Cameron had been there with us.

"He's showing me something like a church—your church or your spirituality—shutting down or changing in a deep way. He's like, 'don't shut it down.' He comes across really cocky, in-your-face—a teenage kind of energy—like he knows everything and isn't afraid to tell you so."

He never was afraid to tell me exactly what he thought. And here I was meeting with a medium. Talk about my spirituality changing in a deep way! I thought maybe he was asking me not to doubt it, not to allow my skeptical self to sever the connection we had been building and to recognize my own intuitive abilities to connect with him.

"He's giving you dream state connections. At least twice he's come to visit—different from just dreaming, real visits."

I knew for sure this was true. I'd had dreams of him that felt so real. Dreams that I knew were trying to tell me all was well.

"He's showing me a badge. A sheriff or a policeman. You'll get the connection. I'm not sure what it means."

That seemed to fit, given that he'd died in Sheriff Joe's custody. And it didn't seem like a detail Jamie could pull out of the ether.

"He's acknowledging two other kids, so I don't know if you have two other children, but that's what I'm getting. He just acknowledges them."

Now, that seemed to me something that couldn't just be a wild guess or a standard, one-size-fits-all answer. The hits seemed to be increasing to a point that I just couldn't ignore. I'd asked for a clear message, one that I couldn't question, and I was starting to feel as if I'd gotten my answer.

"Angels, angels. Hmmm. Angels all around him."

While this could have been a description of some heavenly realm, I was thinking of my living room full of angels—statues, drawings, books. Of the weeping angel I'd placed upon the box that held his ashes at the top of my living room bookshelf. I had thought this might be something he'd acknowledge. I was beginning to let down my skeptical guard.

"Happy birthday," Jamie continued. "Two birthdays close together. One a birthday, one an anniversary—very close together and close to today."

His birthday and the anniversary of his death were only a month apart: April 2nd and May 3rd. I had just passed the one-year mark a month ago. Again, for someone who knew nothing of my story, this was too true to be ignored.

"He's very intelligent. Extremely intelligent, but he played that down while he was here. He's not bragging, just acknowledging this."

It seemed very true to me. I'd often suspected that Cameron knew much more than I did, despite his apparent failures in this lifetime. And now he'd strung together a conversation that was answering my New Year's Eve plea to give me a clear message that I couldn't question.

"Two dogs," Jamie said, introducing the topic that would seal my certainty that Cameron was truly here speaking to me. "Do you have two dogs?"

I gave a hesitant nod, although I was thinking that I only had one now. Poor Maia had been put to sleep just last month and Cheyenne was left all alone.

"One of them is with him, he's showing me," Jamie continued. "The darker dog. I'm getting an 'M' name. The other dog, the one that's here, she still plays with the darker dog. So when you see her acting goofy, she's playing with the other one. The dog that's with him? Did you have to put her to sleep? He says it's okay, you did good. It feels like you might still be healing from this, too."

Wow. This would be awfully hard to guess. Was Maia the "M" name, the one Cameron said was with him at the very beginning of the session? How in the world could anyone guess all those details? Her death was so recent, I *was* still healing from it. She *was* the darker dog, a blue merle to Cheyenne's red. And quite often Cheyenne did act like she was playing all by herself in the yard. It had been a difficult decision to put Maia down. I'd tried so many things before I could finally bring myself to do it, but she was suffering and I couldn't bear it anymore. Cameron was telling me it was the right choice and that she was there with him, but still here, too. Still companioning Cheyenne.

The tears came like a waterfall now, a mixture of sadness and gratitude and awe. If ever I needed a clear answer, how could I

The Medium

deny what I was hearing? There was no way someone could make this stuff up and be so on target with the truth.

As the tears fell, Jamie said, "He's giving you a big hug. He's like a best friend to you. You didn't always understand him, but he understands you completely. He loves you, but he won't cut you any slack. He wants you to be there for yourself like you always were for him. He's showing me caretaker energy. You take care of everyone else, but you need to take care of you."

Since my mother's kidney failure and my dad's two strokes this had certainly been true. And now, with David's accident, there was someone else to worry about. I felt like I *was* taking care of myself, but maybe from his perspective I was spreading myself too thin. I could almost feel Cameron's hug and concern and I felt overwhelmed by it.

"A new blouse, new clothes," Jamie continued, changing the tone of the conversation.

I giggled. "Is he the one helping me to find all the good deals?" I asked, remembering the string of amazing fashion bargains I'd been finding ever since Cameron had died. I'd never had such luck finding clothes I loved at bargain prices in my life.

"Yes, he's the one. You're finding the things you love. Nobody else even sees them. Because they're invisible and then, bang, you can see them and they're just right for you. He's doing that for you."

There was a pause as I absorbed this information, then Jamie asked, "Do you have any questions you want to ask?"

"What about the things from the beach?" I asked, thinking of the series of heart-shaped stones and shells I'd been finding every time I went to a beach and thought about Cameron.

"The things from the beach. Yes, those are from him. He says, 'You're really slow sometimes, Mom.' Yes. There were two or three different things and those were from him."

My heart was beating hard as I asked the question that Cameron's friend had triggered in my mind just before the end of the year. "Do we know the whole story about what happened?"

"No. You don't know everything. What you've been told isn't the whole picture. Your intuition is more correct than what you think you 'know'."

All the turmoil over what I should do bubbled up in me. Should I have filed a wrongful death suit right off the bat? Should I open an investigation now? Did I sell Cameron out by not investigating his death right away?

"Does he want me to do anything about it?" I asked, hesitantly.

"No! Whoosh," Jamie said, waving his hands in front of him. "Let it be. Let it be. I'm getting that it came out sort of like he might have taken his own life or that it was his fault. He says, 'It wasn't all me. All the stuff that happened, it wasn't all because of me. But let it be. Let it go. Don't let it eat you up.' Yes, he was in a frustrated state of mind, but he did not cause everything that happened to him. But he wants you to let it go."

I felt such relief at that, because it just wasn't in me to sue or seek vengeance. No matter what I might do, it wouldn't bring him back. But I didn't want him to think I didn't care or that I was letting him down all over again. It seemed that we were on the same page and that letting it go was best for both of us.

Jamie let out a big, deep sigh and said, speaking for Cameron, "I love you, Mom. I'm okay. Let it go."

I was in emotional overload. I stopped to wipe my eyes and blow my nose.

When Jamie spoke again, he said, "He wants you to listen to the music. He has two or three songs that he connects to you with. He wants you to listen and know that's him talking."

Ever since his funeral, I'd been hearing a couple of the tunes I'd played at the service on the radio. They seemed to play whenever I was thinking of Cameron or whenever I was making choices that were self-nurturing. I'd wondered if that was him. And then there was that tune that came on New Year's Eve as I'd begged him for a message.

"Your work is changing. There's a lull or a shift going on. He's showing me your hands, something about your hands and healing. Somehow you'll be healing with your hands. He wants you to know he has energy, too, and he'll be helping you."

I wondered about that, about what it might mean. I was deeply comforted by the thought that he would be with me in whatever my work might become.

"He's there, right there behind you, rubbing your back," Jamie said. "I get that he does that a lot. 'Heal yourself first,' he says. 'The rest of it will come. See things how you want them to be, not as they appear to be.'"

Our hour was over and I had an awful lot to absorb. I was glad I'd taken notes, because I'd never be able to remember all that was said otherwise. As I left Jamie's house and drove home, it hadn't yet sunk in just how completely Cameron had answered the specific questions I'd asked in my New Year's Eve journaling.

I'd asked to know that he was okay and that was the first thing he'd said to me through Jamie. I'd asked if he was there when David crashed the four-wheeler, and the accident was brought up and acknowledged in the session. I'd asked for clear communication that I wouldn't be able to dismiss and he'd fed Jamie details that only he could know: that there were two siblings, that there were two dogs and one was now with him, and so many other things. I couldn't help but believe this communication had been real.

The only question that wasn't answered was what we had come here to do together and whether we'd accomplished it. Maybe that's a question I can't know the answer to until my life is over and the contract I created for myself this time around is once again made clear to me. But he had said he'd be lending his energy to my work. So maybe, even though he was gone, our work together was not over.

Turning Point

My visit with the medium marked a powerful turning point in my journey. Suddenly any doubt about there being an afterlife, or about Cameron's wellbeing, was lifted. I felt more solidly at peace than at any point during the previous year. It's not that all the sorrow suddenly disappeared, but it was now softened by the sure knowledge that his life was continuing in some other dimension and form. What had been a theoretical belief was now, to me, indisputable truth. Cameron was still alive and we were still connected.

The night after meeting with Jamie, I dreamed.

June 2, 2005 — He's Not Dead After All

A friend of Cameron's comes to the door and starts to tell me something, perhaps to offer his condolences. But I interrupt him and say, "Cameron's at work right now, but I'll tell him you stopped by when he gets back." The young man looks really stunned, like I've lost my mind. I see the look on his face and I rush to say, "Oh! I'm sorry! No one's told you yet. He's not dead after all. It was just a big mixup." Then I remember my family is here — my sister and my Mom — I haven't explained it to them yet, either.

The dream felt right to me. He wasn't really dead. Not in the way we've been taught to think of death. He was just off at work, continuing to learn and grow and further his soul's journey. But when it came to telling people about my new point of view, I was not as straightforward in waking life as I had been in my dream. I never even told David I'd gone to see a medium. I did share the experience with a few friends. Although I felt uncomfortable

Turning Point

sharing this new certainty with my family, I imagine the shift in me must have been obvious.

New energy bubbled up in me and I felt ready to move forward in my life. The timing was perfect, as life coach training began just a few days after my session with Jamie. It was as if the paving stones were being laid before me feet just as I was ready to take each new step. I couldn't see where the path would take me, but I was beginning to trust that the next step would always be there for me as long as I continued to move.

During the first weekend session of life coach training, I could feel the strong synergy between coaching and CJEA. It seemed like coaching would be the perfect vehicle for delivering CJEA's transformative tools and practices to clients in a very empowering way. And, as with CJEA, it was clear that in order to learn how to coach others, I would first have to be coached through my own stuff along the way.

In one of the opening activities our teacher, KC Miller, asked for a volunteer and I surprised myself by raising my hand. She wanted to demonstrate a tool called the Wheel of Balance, which helps to identify the areas in one's life that are most in need of attention and improvement. She began by asking me a little about myself and one of the first questions she asked was how many children I had.

Well, now that's a tricky question. Should I say two, thereby denying Cameron's existence? Or should I say three, knowing that the next questions will undoubtedly lead to the fact of his death? There is nothing closer to social suicide than to bring up the death of a loved one in mixed company. People become very uncomfortable and don't know what to say. It's a real conversation stopper.

I took a deep breath and said, "Three," hoping she'd move on to something else.

"Oh, three. How nice. And how old are they?"

Shit. What should I say now? Was he 26, eternally? Was he 27, as he would have been on his last birthday? Putting off the inevitable, I began with the youngest child.

"My son, Ryan, is 18. My daughter, Sarah, is 24. And my oldest, Cameron, would be 27, but he died about a year ago." There, it was out. In front of a whole room full of strangers who would now not know what to say to me as we spent the next several months together in training. How awkward. *Please, God, don't let me cry. I do not want to go there today.*

"He's here with you today," she said. "I feel his presence really strongly all around you."

Well, that was a bit unexpected. But suddenly I didn't feel so much like I was in a room full of strangers as that I was in a room full of likeminded friends.

"I hope that he is," I said.

"And you're a good mother," KC continued.

"Well, I don't know how good a mother I am. I know I've made a lot of mistakes."

"And you're a good mother," she repeated, looking me in the eye and smiling brightly.

"Well, I suppose I've been a better mother for the younger two than I ever was for Cameron," I compromised, thinking about his troubled life and death.

"And you're a good mother," she insisted once again.

I'm not sure how many times she repeated that statement as I continued to contradict her and sell myself short. Finally, her smiling insistence wore me down.

"I know that I've always tried to be the best mother I knew how to be," I conceded. "And I've loved each of my children with all my heart."

It felt very good to say that out loud, as if the breath that carried the words out of me also carried away a bit of my guilt, regret and self-doubt. KC beamed at me, nodding emphatically to support my budding self-acceptance.

Life coaching is like that. It's all about helping people to discover and accept their greatness and goodness and personal power. It's about helping to steer them away from the knee-jerk reactions of unhelpful habits, old stories and self-deprecating talk.

As we went on with the actual Wheel of Balance exercise, KC handed me a diagram of a circle divided into pie-shaped wedges, each labeled with an aspect of life: relationships, health, work, spirituality, and others. She handed me some colored markers and asked me to rate my satisfaction in each area by coloring in a portion of its representative pie wedge. A tiny bit filled in would mean little satisfaction and a fully colored wedge would mean great satisfaction.

She then asked me to choose which area I'd most like to improve. I chose "fun and recreation," not because it was the lowest scoring area, but because it felt like the safest area to explore in this public forum. For the next few minutes, KC prompted me with questions that challenged me to sort out my thoughts and feelings around this area of my life.

I was surprised, in the course of the coaching, how much emotion was there, just under the surface, waiting to be expressed. I knew that the loss of Cameron had taken a toll on me and on my relationship with David. I so longed for fun and happiness to come back into our lives. The quads had been a nice start, but since the accident I was afraid to get back on them. And even though it had been more than six months since that awful day, David's injuries were still painful. Something as physical as four-wheeling was out of the question for now.

I knew that my introspective nature and private grieving process, along with David's reluctance to discuss Cameron's death, were creating a wedge between us just as surely as Cameron had while he was alive. I wanted to be free of that, to be friends and have fun together like we did in our early years. Our interests were different in so many ways that the challenge would be to find some common ground where we could meet to play. It seemed like traveling together might be a way to do that. I resolved to talk to David about finding ways to have fun together. In just a few minutes of simple coaching I was already feeling new energy and seeing new possibilities.

Heading home from training that day, as I got into my car and started the engine, "Love Is" was playing on the radio. I had played this duet about the healing power of love at Cameron's funeral service. And the very next song to come on the radio was Stevie Wonder's "As," another song I'd played at the funeral. This undeniable synchronicity seemed to confirm to me what KC had said: that Cameron was present with me. I felt that he was telling me the steps I'd taken today (embarking on this training, claiming the truth of having been a good mother, and exploring ways to put fun and joy back into my life) were good steps and he was supporting me. Perhaps he was even guiding me.

It wasn't the first time he'd seemed to speak to me through the car radio and it wouldn't be the last. As Jamie had said, "He wants you to listen to the music . . . and know that's him talking."

Speak to Me in Music

Ever since Cameron had died, he'd been speaking to me through music. As had happened after that first day of life coaching, I'd been noticing that I'd hear one of "our" songs whenever I was on the right track in my life, whenever I was doing something nurturing for myself or something that would help me to heal and to grow.

At first Cameron got my attention by using songs that were in my mind and heart, the ones I'd played at his service, but after a while I started talking to him while I drove and asking him questions. I'd listen to whatever song would come on next and it would often hold an answer to my question. It seemed he could speak to me through the music.

One night on the way home from life coaching class, I pulled onto the freeway, turned on the radio and said to Cameron, "Talk to me baby, I'm listening."

I started thinking about the mechanics of it all. How could he control the radio? Could he plant a thought in the DJ's mind to play a particular tune? What if Cameron's busy with something else where he is? How could he be here fiddling with my car radio and still be wherever he is, doing whatever he's doing? Then I started thinking about all the people who love me and how they hold a little part of me in their hearts, and all the people that I love who I hold in my heart.

I had this mental image of connecting streams of light, like lighted wires, connecting all of us. Through these cords of love, some token of my own light resides in all those hearts even while I'm out here driving down the freeway. I thought, yes, it is possible. It's happening right now as I drive. By virtue of all those who love me and all those I love, I am in multiple places at once. Why couldn't he be? There is something that connects us and that something is love. Perhaps the speed of love is even more instantaneous than the speed of light.

Right after that revelation struck me, what came on the radio was Michael McDonald's rendition of "Ain't No Mountain High Enough." Cameron couldn't have picked a better song to confirm what I was thinking and to assure me he was there. The song starts with "Listen baby..." echoing my appeal of "Talk to me baby." The refrain of "ain't no mountain high enough, ain't no valley low enough, ain't no river wide enough to keep me from gettin' to you" seemed to be telling me that even death was no obstacle. He could be with me whenever I called. And when the words, "My love is alive" were sung, I felt a thrill of recognition that love *does* survive death.[42] It's a cord that can't be severed.

Over time, other songs have become messages that pass between Cameron and me. Always they seem to reflect what I've been puzzling over or working out in my new understanding of a continuing relationship after death.

India.Arie's version of the old Don Henley song, "The Heart of the Matter," began to play on the radio often while I was working hard at self-forgiveness. Even though it's a breakup song, the lyrics seemed to match what I was feeling: that even when there's no way to put things back together the way they were, we still need forgiveness to be free.[43] Learning to live without Cameron involved forgiving him and forgiving myself.

Seal is another artist that both Cameron and I liked. When Seal's "Love's Divine" began getting air play recently, I found the lyrics reflected my new awareness that love is all that's important in this life. A song about healing, forgiveness and the redeeming value of love, the first time I heard it I thought about Cameron and felt he understood that no matter what may have happened in our lives together, my love never wavered.[44] Love is, underneath it all, who we are. I felt that through this song, Cameron was trying to tell me my love had helped him to know who he was.

The tendency might be to dismiss these kinds of incidents as wishful thinking or to explain them away by saying that I'm hearing what I want to hear. I think it's more than that. Music and the words of song create a kind of living dream. The artists that craft the words and notes are tapping into the same realm from which dreams spring. The distance between the living and the dead is not vast; our departed are close as breath to us. When we lose someone with whom we were very entangled, it's as if the door between here and there is left open a crack, and our thoughts and feelings slip in and out between the realms. Dreams, music, poetry, meditational journeys—these gain the easiest passage and so become a medium for message exchange.

String of Pearls

Guided meditation was a tool we used over and over again in the life coaching training program. It's a process in which a voice guides you, with a story and imagery, into a meditative state that is a bit like dreaming. During the course of the training, there were three meditational experiences in particular that were very powerful for me.

In the first of these, we were asked to envision ourselves on another plane, looking out across the Universe and seeing this lovely little blue planet in the distance.

The teacher guided us in her soft voice, ". . . and now a longing fills you to come to this place, to heal it. You sense you have a job to do and slowly, slowly, you drift in closer to the planet, looking down upon its beautiful blues and greens. As you descend ever closer, you begin to decide just where you will be born. You choose a location and you choose the parents who will bring you into this world. And you drift in closer and, at the right moment, you plant your spirit into the body that will carry you into this world. . . ."

The meditation continued, assuring us that as we arrived upon this planet we would learn and absorb everything we needed to in order to do the job we came to do. We would meet the right people and recognize each other. We would change the world.

It was a moving meditation, and I felt empowered by it. However, what was most meaningful to me came through the comments others had about their experience during the meditation in relation to choosing their parents.

One gentleman was moved to tears as he shared his realization that even though his relationship with his parents had not been a good one, he'd still pick the same ones, because they made him who he is. Through his trials with them he'd become strong and compassionate and ready to help others.

Another woman spoke about the longing she'd had during the meditation to truly be able to come back, to choose the same parents and to start anew. She wished she had done more for her parents, been more for them. She hoped she'd be able to be with them again in a future life so she could give them all the love she'd withheld from them this time around.

Between these two stories, a glimmer of new understanding dawned in me regarding Cameron. First, I was overcome by the idea that he *chose us* to be his parents. Beyond that was the recognition that maybe we did just what we were supposed to do—just what he *needed* us to do—in order to fulfill his own mission here, whatever that may have been.

Neither of those ideas was brand new to me, but when I heard the passion in the voices of these two people speaking about their parents, the concepts sunk in to a more visceral level and became more real to me. I'd always felt there was a strong karmic bond between Cameron, David and me. Maybe despite the apparent tragedy of his death, we had accomplished what we were meant to accomplish together. It was hard to imagine what that might have been. Yet as the gentleman had expressed, despite the struggles, his parents had made him who he was and he was grateful for that.

A third feeling washed over me, and this was new and a little overwhelming. Perhaps it wasn't even about what we did or didn't do for him. Maybe Cameron had come here to do something for *us*. Maybe through all the heartache and pain, he'd been working to give us a gift, to help us evolve. I felt humbled by the thought and so grateful for the gift he'd been in my life.

In a later meditation, we were guided to a party of celebration, an affair at which each of us was the guest of honor. We were to be fêted for all of our life's accomplishments. At one point in this meditation, I was walking down a red carpet toward a big door. "As the door swings wide, you are greeted by a shining, smiling face," said the voice guiding me.

As I saw that door swing wide, Cameron was there, smiling broadly, welcoming me with a big bear hug. It was so real. I'd never been that good at this meditation stuff. I'd never really *seen* much as the hypnotist's voice guided me. Sometimes I'd have vague feelings which my left brain would quickly dismiss as make-believe. But this was *real*.

It felt like the dreams I'd had that were more than dreams. It felt like truly being in Cameron's presence. He was the first in line to congratulate me and thank me for having been a great Mom to him. There was immense healing in that moment. And the distance between us, between the here and the hereafter, seemed to shrink down to nothing.

Several times after this meditation during the remaining months of training, I had dreams in which I had long, substantive conversations with Cameron. I could never quite remember the content of our conversations in the morning, but gone were the tears and the anger. I was no longer pushing him away in my dreams. We were communicating, and I was healing.

The months of life coach training would do much to quicken the healing process. Since the training was hands-on, we practiced by coaching each other. I would benefit from hours and hours of coaching to help me through my grief and to find my way toward my contribution to this world.

Toward the end of the life coaching training program, we were guided through another meditation. This time, we were asked to see ourselves approaching a canvas and choosing any colors we desired to create our own unique work of art. This work of art was the canvas of our lives and our contribution to the world. After my meditational experience, I journaled, trying to capture in words all I had seen, heard and felt.

> *My canvas has no boundaries. Rays of color flow out and out from the center. I am at the center. I become a spider, weaving, weaving—the rays become warp and I weave the weft, rainbow colored threads spiraling round and round and ever outward. No boundaries. Beads, too, of rainbow colors—and then I hear the Michael Franks song:*

String of Pearls

> Suddenly, the Rainbow
> Hits us from a different angle
> Suddenly, our hearts know
> Love's the thread on which we dangle
> Shining like a string of pearls
> All our hearts held together
> Like a string of pearls[45]

And I know that I am weaving love and connecting hearts—or really just finding the connections that are already there and bringing them to life. And the spiral will never stop growing. Leading people to their own hearts and through them to their own connection to the web and all the others on it. And to their own greatness—all of us shining like a string of pearls, a rainbow web of love.

I was reminded of the image I'd had in my mind when I was trying to figure out how Cameron could be with me through a song on the radio even though he was in a different dimension and presumably busy with other things, the image of our hearts all being connected by lighted wires or streams of light. The rainbow web was another way of seeing those connections, and in the rainbow web, I had an active role to play in weaving those connections and bringing them to life.

Agreements

It seemed clear that Cameron and I were still connected, perhaps had always been connected. I felt that our roots ran much deeper than just this lifetime. There had been a constant undercurrent of drama and unresolved pain that seemed out of proportion with the actual events of our lives. It was as if rather than the events of our lives having created all the emotional turmoil, the emotional turmoil had come in with us and shaped and molded our interactions.

There had always been a disconcerting, three-way, energetic tug-of-war between David, Cameron and me. There was a constant tension so thick between us that it was almost visible. David and I had disagreements over the other two children in the course of raising them, but never with the overpoweringly charged emotions that came up around Cameron.

Through the years, I'd puzzled over exactly what had drawn our souls together this time around. I'd even tried to do a past life regression with a hypnotherapist some time back in the 90's, without any success.

As the therapist counted me down and back in time, a big wall came up in me. It was a barrier that would not let me through. I started to cry uncontrollably. When he asked what the tears were about, I couldn't explain it. There was just this unfathomable well of sadness.

After trying a few more times at home, with regression cassette tapes, I finally gave up. I came to the conclusion that whatever had occurred in our past lives together, something didn't want me to know about it in this life. I didn't know whether that something was a fear in me or some outside entity who deemed it was not in my best interest.

Still, I knew we must have shared a past and that we must have made some agreement to come together again. Perhaps karma had brought us together either to heal us or to punish us for past transgressions.

Agreements

Numerologically, I was surprised (and yet not surprised) to learn that Cameron, David and I each shared 31/4 as our "life path number." The number is calculated by adding together all of the digits of one's birth date, and I found it quite interesting that all three of our birthdays would add up to the same number—31. In numerology, you always keep adding until you reach a single digit, so our primary number ended up "4." A "4" as one's primary number has to do with stability and step-by-step progress, the "3" is about expression and sensitivity, and the "1" reflects creativity and confidence. The positive manifestation of the 31/4 life path could mean success in reaching any life goal with self-confidence, creativity, balanced emotions, planning, patience and follow-through. The shadow aspects of each number, though, could lead to self-doubt, insecurity, disappointment, depression, instability, impatience, confusion and a feeling of stuckness that could lead to addiction.[46] While David and I had each struggled with these shadows to some degree, it seemed that Cameron had lived them out in spades.

Now that Cameron was gone, my curiosity about our karmic connections resurfaced. I thought it was possible that while it would not have served me to know what our agreement was for this lifetime while Cameron was alive, maybe now the record could be opened. Through the AZHCC, I had met a woman, Dorothy Neddermeyer, Ph.D., who specialized in regression therapy, both for healing childhood traumas and for exploring past lives.[47] I decided to make an appointment with her.

My first session with Dr. Neddermeyer was disappointing, because I wanted to jump right into a past life, while Dorothy suggested that I should simply try to talk to Cameron first. I understood from reading about regression work that it's important to clear issues from the current life before going back farther, but I was impatient to sort out my karmic history with Cameron. I wanted to control the direction of our session together, but I deferred to Dorothy's expertise.

She wanted to help me reach a hypnotic state in which I could speak to Cameron where he was now. In a future session, she promised, we would try to go back to a past life together.

As she guided me and counted me down, I felt that block wall come up again just as it had so many years ago. What was it in me that so resisted this? As she asked me what I saw and whether Cameron was there, I kept telling her I didn't see anything. I was very frustrated.

Through her gentle questioning I eventually started crying. What surfaced was my sense of the waste Cameron's death represented to me—the waste of his potential. As we talked about this, now with no pretense of being under hypnosis, it somehow became apparent (whether by my own recognition or Dorothy's suggestion, I don't recall) that it was not really Cameron's potential being wasted at this point, but my own. He, in the afterlife, was living out his full potential, while I was the one feeling stuck and unable to move forward in my life.

I could see the truth in that. Since I'd completed my life coaching training, I'd had all kinds of ideas for building a practice but seemed never to have the energy to move forward with them. I kept thinking I was ready to move forward and to let go of all this grief, but the tears still came too easily.

"It sounds like part of where you are stuck might be your inability to forgive yourself," Dorothy suggested.

I balked at that and argued that I *had* forgiven myself and I was no longer carrying the kind of guilt I had carried at first. Even as I argued, though, I felt she might be right. There was a part of me that felt I didn't deserve a successful and happy life since Cameron couldn't have one.

I drove home from the session feeling frustrated and unhappy. I'd hoped for some kind of an amazing revelation from a past life that would suddenly make sense of everything. Instead I felt like I'd ended up right where I started: depressed and stuck. At the time, I wasn't sure I'd go back for another session. I guess I was looking for a quick fix, but if that's what I really wanted I could have gone to a traditional therapist and gotten a prescription for Prozac.

In retrospect, I know that Dorothy was taking me exactly where I needed to go. It was my own stubbornness and impatience that kept getting in the way.

Agreements

The next morning, one of the subscription emails in my inbox carried the title "Learning to Forgive."[48] Given the topic of the previous day's session, the title jumped out at me. The story as a whole didn't feel relevant to me, but one paragraph in particular grabbed my attention. It was about how *accepting* forgiveness requires remorse, but forgiving itself doesn't. By forgiving someone, you can let go of the weight you are carrying whether the offending party ever feels remorse or not.

What that triggered in me was the "A-ha!" that in *self-forgiveness*, I was both the forgiver and the one accepting the forgiveness. I wondered which part of me had not yet done its job. Had the forgiver-self been waiting for the transgressor-self to show enough remorse before extending forgiveness? Or had the forgiver-self extended forgiveness, but the transgressor-self not been willing to accept it? I certainly had felt immense remorse, but had I been willing to let it go? Maybe a *part* of accepting forgiveness was feeling remorse, but maybe the final step was letting that remorse go. Wasn't forgiveness supposed to be an act of grace? Wasn't forgiveness supposed to wash away our sins? If I truly did forgive myself, then wasn't it time to let go of the guilt?

I decided to meet with Dorothy again, and I told her about the synchronicity of the forgiveness email. She said that maybe what we ought to do this time would be to try to talk to Cameron about forgiveness and to find out what *he* thought. He might even be able to help me to accept forgiveness from him and from myself. It was not really where I wanted to go, but I agreed to give it a try. I was beginning to see that where I felt the most resistance was usually exactly where I needed to go.

Before she began the hypnosis, she talked to me a little bit about what had been going on in my life since we last met. I told her that part of where I felt so stuck was in my home office, which used to be Cameron's bedroom. I told her it was always so cluttered and disorganized that I couldn't think straight. Every time I thought about trying to clean it up, I just got overwhelmed. I joked that sometimes I blamed it on Cameron, as though his ADHD energy was trapped in that room and I'd inherited it by osmosis. I wondered, too, whether, in some crazy way, I might be trying to fill the void his death had left by recreating some of his drama and dysfunction in my own workspace.

I had been thinking lately that maybe the way we could best honor our departed loved ones was by healing in ourselves what we saw as broken in them and embracing in ourselves everything we saw as bright and beautiful in them. I wondered if it was time for me to reconcile my own tendencies toward disorganization, laziness and addiction and to embrace the part of me that, like Cameron, simply marched to its own drumbeat.

This time, the hypnosis was a bit more effective. The wall of resistance did not appear right away. Dorothy instructed me to find a place where I could meet with Cameron, and I saw myself in my office just as it was: messy piles of paper everywhere, projects started and abandoned, books and art supplies teetering on every surface. I saw Cameron in the doorway. He gave me a big hug. The tears began, and I said aloud, "I am not doing this anymore! I'm not going to waste this time on tears. We are together. Let's talk."

I asked him, "What am I going to do about this mess?" and he just grinned. How many times had I asked that very same question of him about his own messes?

Dorothy reminded me that I was sidestepping the issue of forgiveness. As soon as she said that, I no longer felt Cameron's presence and I felt like I'd snapped back into her office.

I told her as much and she said, "That's okay. What comes up for you when you think of forgiveness?"

"Letting go. Peace. Acceptance," I replied.

"What do you think blocks it?"

I had a very full sense of *exactly* what blocked it, but I couldn't quite describe it. I could only say, "Expectations."

"Of what?" she prompted.

"Of how things should be." As I said it, I had a strong sense of Cameron mentally pushing me to realize that that was exactly what I needed to let go of.

Dorothy asked, "And how *should* things be?"

"There shouldn't be all this pain and suffering. Kids shouldn't die. Parents should know what the hell they're doing. It shouldn't be so hard to do what we came here to do!" I said, nearly shouting.

I was feeling overwhelming anger now, and something more than that. Disillusionment. Disbelief. Incredulity. I felt I'd been duped.

What I said aloud was, "I can't believe I would have agreed to this—that I signed up for this!"

Dorothy pointed out that maybe I didn't sign up for it, or that maybe I couldn't see how it would turn out when I'd signed up for it. Maybe Cameron and I had just agreed to work on something together, not knowing how it would turn out. She reminded me that 'shit happens' and suggested the possibility that things had just happened, without our having agreed to it at all.

I left feeling frustrated again—not with Dorothy, but with myself. I was tired of all the tears, tired of wanting to be done with this grief, tired of thinking that I *was* done with it, only to find over and over again that I wasn't. I wanted to know what Cameron and I had come here to do and whether we'd done it. It seemed like the only thing that would bring me peace.

So what had we agreed to work on? I mulled it over as I drove home. On the radio, Seal sang about forgiveness and the divinity of love.[49]

Tangled Threads

When I met with Dorothy for the third time, she agreed to regress me to the place and time in which Cameron and I had made our agreement for this lifetime. It was a much longer hypnosis process this time. I found I was able to visualize some things, but my visualizations were out of synch with Dorothy's guidance. She told me to see myself going downstairs, and I saw a curved metal and concrete staircase on the outside of a building, going down to a beach. "Now you're in a hallway going toward a door," she continued.

Since I was outdoors in my reverie, my hallway was a kind of lanai, like the lanais in my elementary school, and the door was industrial metal with a pushbar handle and a frosted glass window. I could see light through the window, but nothing else. When I opened the door, I was in a school hallway lined with lockers. "When you open the door, you find yourself in a meadow," said the voice.

My mind registered that she'd been walking me from the inside out while I'd been journeying the reverse path—from the outside in. After a moment of disorientation, I was able to place myself in a meadow and find a bench to sit on. I could even feel the breeze and smell the fresh air. "Look up over your right shoulder and you'll see a thread—a silver thread," she said.

I didn't see a thread or sense one and I lost all of the visualization I'd been able to sustain up to this point. I started to see instead great balls of color rolling inside my eyelids. Purple mostly. When I reported this to her, she took me out and started to count me down deeper.

The colors began to cycle through: purple, red, orange, yellow. I found a ladder to climb and the voice instructed me to climb through the colors and into the mist. "When you're through all the colors," she said, "find yourself in a location and when you've found a place to sit, tell me where you are."

I saw a beach. I sat on a log by the sea.

"Now, invite Cameron to come sit with you."

I couldn't see him, but I could feel him sitting by me, shoulder to shoulder, like buddies, like old friends.

"Now, ask him to go with you to the place and time where you met to discuss your agreement for this lifetime," Dorothy instructed. "Listen carefully to what you are saying to each other."

All I had was a sense that we were both happy. I couldn't get any context. Then the colors began again. More yellow now, a small purple circle surrounded by yellow light, and then the yellow just filled everything up.

"What comes up for you when you think of yellow?" she asked.

"I think of the chakras, but I think that's just my mind intellectualizing."

"Maybe," she said. "Or maybe there's something about the chakras you need to know and the yellow is bringing that up. So what is the yellow chakra?"

"Personal power," I said.

"Please ask Cameron to step aside for a moment—there's something else I need to do right now, but I'll come back to him in a moment," she said.

"I think he's already gone, anyway," I replied.

Dorothy surprised me by saying, "I see three guides with you right now, two males and a female. I want you to ask one of them to come forth and help you with personal power."

I felt and saw the shape of an angel—a female. What came up for me was "Grace," both as a name and a concept. I seemed to receive a message. "Be aware of Grace, pay attention to it. Trust. You are safe. Trust in the unfolding. Impatience gets in your way. Fear gets in your way." I felt as though my connection to Grace had been eternal, that I'd been forever under her protection.

As I was experiencing this connection with Grace, Dorothy had been picking up other information from my trio of guides. What they told her was that I didn't need to remember the commitment I'd made to Cameron. I needed to remember the commitment I'd made to myself.

After she brought me back out of hypnosis, we discussed this information from my guides. Dorothy suggested that while Cameron might know what we came here to do, he might know it only from his own spiritual perspective, which might not be of use to me. Or he might realize it would not be in my best interest for him to tell me. At any rate, my guides seemed to be steering me away from gaining that knowledge.

It put me in mind of one of C. S. Lewis' stories in *The Chronicles of Narnia*. In the story called "The Horse and His Boy," the main character, Shasta, finds himself traveling in the company of a runaway princess named Aravis.

Aravis had tricked one of her servants and then drugged her in order to escape from an arranged marriage. At one point as she travels with Shasta, Aravis is stalked and then clawed by a great lion. Later, Shasta meets the lion and discovers that he is the Great Aslan, the creator and protector god of Narnia.

When Aravis eventually meets Aslan, he tells her that he striped her back with his claws so that she would know the pain her servant felt when she was whipped for helping her to run away. Aravis is filled with remorse and begs Aslan to tell her if any further harm has come to the slave since. But Aslan replies by saying, "Child, I am telling you your story, not hers. No one is told any story but their own."[50]

Perhaps Cameron's story and my story were so completely entangled that by learning more of my own, too much of his would be revealed. Or perhaps the time was not yet right for me to know too much of my own story.

I thought about a fantasy trilogy I'd recently read called *His Dark Materials*, by Philip Pullman.[51] The heroine in that story, Lyra, has a great destiny before her but she must not be allowed to learn what it is. It must unfold for her through free choice, or it won't really be destiny at all.

The Kidnap of Personal Power

A few weeks after that third meeting with Dr. Neddermeyer, I had a dream that seemed relevant to personal power.

> ***February 21, 2006 — Protecting my Yellow Car***
>
>
>
> *I have a yellow car – a very racy sports car. I've just parked it, when some young kids come up and ooh and aah over it. One kid reaches out to touch the fender and I start yelling at them to leave my car alone. I'm sure they are going to vandalize it. I think I beat one kid up. I threaten to kill any one of them that touches my car.*

Upon awakening, I was shocked at the intensity of my anger in the dream. These little children were not truly going to vandalize anything. They were simply in awe of my shiny, powerful car. Why I'd felt compelled to beat them up and threaten them with death was beyond me in waking life.

When I next met with Dorothy, I told her about the dream.

"What age were the kids in the dream?" she asked.

"I don't know. Not real little," I said. "I guess about nine or ten."

"This may be reflecting something that happened to you at the age of nine or ten," she said.

I argued with her. The dream could mean any number of things and the age of the kids was not even spelled out in it. I felt very defensive, as a matter of fact. *Don't tell me what my dream means, I'm a dream expert and that's not how it's done*, I thought. I didn't say it aloud, though, because I knew that I was overreacting. There must have been something to what she was saying for her suggestion to trigger such a defensive response. Years of dreamwork had taught me that we are often blind to what our dreams are telling us when it's something we'd rather not know. She'd hit a nerve and I wasn't sure what it was all about. Apparently I didn't want to know, because my resistance continued.

"I only bring the dream up because of the yellow car," I said, trying to deflect her away from my childhood. "It seems to represent personal power, a concern that came up in our last session."

"The dream comes up now," she persisted, "because it's saying that some event that happened when you were nine or ten is related to your current feelings of being disempowered."

"When my own kids were nine or ten," I recalled, "I used to just lose it with them. It was like the anger I had in the dream. They would do something totally inconsequential and this rage would just boil up in me. It wasn't quite as physical as in the dream, I didn't beat them up, but it was the same kind of irrational and disproportional response to some minor infraction."

"Interesting," she said. "But it was the fact that your kids were nine or ten that triggered that anger in you. It's still related to when you were nine or ten."

She suggested regressing me to the age of nine or ten to see what memories would arise. I was annoyed with the suggestion, thinking how far off track we were getting from my initial desire to do a past life regression. But I agreed to make that exploration and I told myself that whatever came up would be for my healing and best interests. I had already gained much from my sessions with her, despite my frustration around not getting to a past life. Dorothy obviously knew what she was doing, and I trusted her direction. I sat back to see where this next path would take me.

At first, as she regressed and guided me to find my nine- or ten-year-old self, nothing much came up. I was trying, intellectually, to figure out some landmarks. What grade would I have been in at nine or ten? Who were my friends? What popped into my head, finally, was a picture of me and my two best childhood friends playing Monopoly.

"What were those games like?" she probed.

"Oh, they were just a lot of fun," I said. "The games would sometimes last the entire day. There's not much coming up around it, no power struggles or anything."

She took me back to my ninth birthday.

I saw and felt nothing.

"How did your family celebrate birthdays?" she asked. "A cake with candles?"

I was disturbed to realize that I had *no memory* of ever sitting in front of a birthday cake to blow out the candles, although I knew that I must have. What I did remember was my mother saying to me that we didn't have birthday parties (the kind where you invite all your little school friends) because that was just begging for presents. It was amazing the depth of emotion I felt in recalling that. It seemed so trivial when I said it aloud, but I suddenly felt so small and sad.

We talked about that a little bit, and I said, "It's all that Catholic crap! You shouldn't want anything or think you're any kind of special. That's just wrong and sinful. It's like you were supposed to just learn to accept that you were worthless."

I felt I was falling into an endless dark pit of sadness. "This goes deep," I said, fighting tears.

"Where in your body do you feel this?" she asked.

"In my throat. Sharp, at the back of my jaw. It's like having to swallow down a bunch of lies when I know the truth. An upward rising pressure. Black. It reminds me of the acid reflux I often experience at night."

"What comes to you when I say fear?" she asked.

"Fear?" I asked. "My whole relationship with Cameron was based on fear."

"And when did you first realize that?" she asked.

"I recognize it now, in retrospect. But maybe I started to realize it in Las Vegas, the night he ran away." I started to cry, remembering that night and the night he sliced his feet over and over again with that broken plastic protractor.

"And when is the first time you were that afraid?" she probed.

I knew she was trying to get me back into childhood memories, but the only things that rose in my mind were all about Cameron. I told her about the time he almost drowned and how responsible, or irresponsible, I'd felt. I cried and cried. I told her about the poem I wrote, "Drowning," and how I always felt I was losing him. I told her about how his whole life long, I was always punishing him for some kind of trouble because I was always afraid of what he'd do next. I tried so hard to control him and keep him boxed in because I was terrified of what he might do to himself. I'd never really let him just be who he was.

It seemed clear to me that I had never let him be his own special self any more than I felt I'd been allowed to be. Why hadn't I realized that the only way to really love Cameron was to accept him just as he was and to try and help him to discover the beauty, strength and light within him? Instead, the message I'd always given him was, "you're broken. Let's fix you." How that must have hurt and stuck in his throat. I suddenly realized that all the pain and alienation I'd ever felt growing up I'd inflicted on him tenfold. It was a heartrending revelation.

I wept then. I wept for Cameron, for myself and for all the little children who have that special light extinguished in them. Not out of any kind of meanness and not even intentionally, but just because that's the way the world works. We come in full of innocence and promise, and the world just squeezes it out of us. We learn that we have no power, because all that's best and brightest in us is so easily taken away.

Looking back, I can see the obvious connection between my own childhood and the pain I felt about Cameron's life. It was as though, in a way, I'd projected my own sense of unworthiness into his life so that I wouldn't have to look at it in my own life. I'm sure this is part of what Dorothy was trying to show me. But I didn't really want to see it.

A few weeks later, I had another dream.

> ### March 15, 2006 — Kidnapping
>
>
>
> *All these young kids are being kidnapped – four-, five-, and six-year olds. There's a creepy old man being questioned and he laughs and he cackles that he's not hurting these children at all. In his eyes, he's rescuing them.*

The dream seemed to reinforce the revelation I'd had in Dorothy's office. It seemed to me that every child in the world gets kidnapped at some point—the Inner Child does. And the perpetrators have no idea, usually, of the damage they are inflicting because it is all done "for your own good."

We spend our whole lives trying to overcome the disempowerment we felt as children. Unfortunately, too often we do that by taking power over the powerless: our own children, the children we teach in school, the children we preach to in church or anyone we perceive as weaker. And so it becomes a vicious cycle with those who were disempowered now disempowering the next generation ad infinitum. Because even though we are adults, we're really just broken little kids trying to raise our own children. It's like the blind leading the blind.

Suddenly I understood more clearly why Dr. Capacchione's Inner Child work was so powerful and important and why Dr. Neddermeyer had persisted in exploring my own childhood before going back to past lives. Everything we see as broken in another is really a reflection of our own inner pain and turmoil.

It seems to me now that all relationship healing is really about healing yourself, forgiving yourself, loving yourself. The only person you can change is *yourself*. But when these inner changes are made—when the inner healing happens—all of your outer relationships change as well.

The true path to personal power involves the ransom of one's own kidnapped Inner Child. When that child is healed and empowered, there is no more need for irrational power struggles with others. When the Inner Child is adequately protected and nurtured, one is no longer ruled by fear.

With Cameron, as with the little kids in the dream of the yellow car, I seemed to always be seeing the worst of intentions rather than the best and anticipating the next infraction before it ever occurred. I was hyper-vigilant about protecting my own power because my Inner Child still felt disempowered. I had mistakenly equated power with control, so when my children were out of control (as Cameron almost always was) my little yellow car was threatened and I lashed out.

But I was beginning to realize that power is not the same as control, and if we think it is we will always be disempowered because control is an illusion. There is really very little in the world we can control. We can influence. We can exercise choice. But we can't control other people or the experiences that will come into our lives. We can only choose, carefully and consciously, how to respond.

Heart Connection

Shortly after the regression work, I had an opportunity to return to Texas for a refresher CJEA training week. Living in Arizona, I don't get a chance to go to the ocean as often as I'd like, so I was almost as excited about visiting South Padre Island again as I was about the intensive.

With all the childhood memories and revelations the regression sessions had brought up, my work at the intensive proved to be powerful and healing. In art, dialogue and journaling, my Inner Child was very evident. At one point, recalling a particularly painful experience from elementary school, I was moved to create a puppet I named Sister Mary Wolfenstein. Her wolf's head protruded from a voluminous black nun's habit, complete with giant rosary and metal ruler (the better to rap your knuckles with!). She represented all the nuns I remembered less than fondly from grade school. My Protective Parent gave her a good talking to for all of the damage inflicted on me as a dreamy little girl in parochial school. And my Nurturing Parent reassured my Inner Child that the sisters had been wrong; I was *not* bad, worthless or stupid.

In another empowering step, I journaled with fear and found that, ultimately, fear was a blowhard. The lesson it was trying to teach me was something I already knew.

(NDH) I am fear and I want to keep you guessing, keep you looking over your shoulder, keep you on the edge. You'll never know when I might show up, when the next shoe's gonna fall. That's the ticket, really. To keep it so you never know. I might jump out of any dark corner or even out of the bright blue sky. You control NOTHING!!!

(DH) I don't like you very much. You seem evil to me in a way. Why do you want to keep me in this state of uncertainty and on edge?

Because you have to understand it–YOU CONTROL NOTHING.

But I can control some things. I am in control of my own life. Yes–death, disease, war, flood and famine happen and yes, I can't control those. But I can control my reactions. I can love and live fully NOW. I don't want to waste my now fearing a later that I don't even know will arrive. You don't scare me anymore and you don't own me anymore!

On a day off from classes, I headed to the beach at South Padre Island. Remembering my last two experiences by the sea, I was anticipating connection and communication with Cameron. All the experiences I'd had over the last year had left me feeling more and more certain that he was only a breath away. Feeling a little cocky, I stepped from the parking lot to the sand and said, "OK, kiddo. I'm here. Where's my gift?"

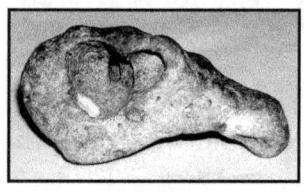

Instantly I found at my feet a stone with the shape of a heart carved nearly all the way through it. I walked that beach all the way down to the end that day and never saw another stone, only shells and seaweed and sand. I was delighted.

Unlike my first two experiences finding the black heart-shaped shell and then the egg-shaped stone with the red heart, this time I wasn't asking from an empty space, a sad space, a longing space. Instead I was asking from a knowing space, a space of expectation, knowing before I ever saw the gift that it would be there for me, knowing in my heart that the connection was there.

The next day, back in my CJEA training session, we were asked to create an illustration of an experience we'd had that week. I drew a picture of myself on the beach, arms up to the sky, the sun shaped like a winged heart. On impulse, I drew a bunch of little hearts in the sand around my feet.

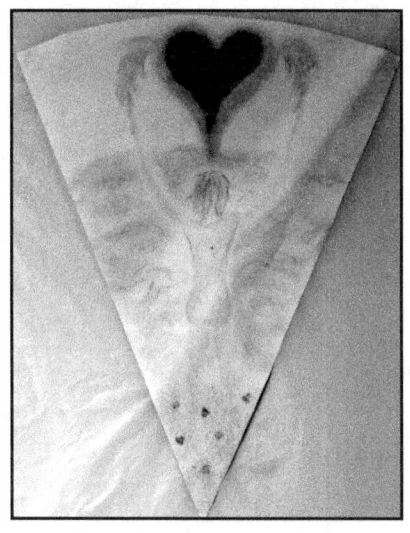

I journaled about my drawing and the three experiences of finding hearts on the beach. I recognized the progressive transformation I'd made over time. The emptiness and longing I'd felt when I visited South Padre that first time and found the little black heart had shifted to a willingness to let go as I created my altar in Puerto Vallarta and now, finally, to a peaceful certainty about the eternal bond I have with my son. I wrote, "I don't have to hold my arms out in longing. His love is all around me all the time." I realized how much healing had occurred since he'd died a little more than year-and-a-half before.

A few months later, I went to Rocky Point, Mexico, with my husband. It was a great, relaxing getaway and I didn't feel any need to look for heart gifts from Cameron. I walked the beach several times, alone and with David, never really even thinking about looking for a heart. On one walk, alone, it crossed my mind that here was yet another step on the healing journey. Not only was I not sadly longing, I didn't even feel the need to ask with expectation. I just knew with no need for confirmation that we were still connected. At that moment, I looked down and all around my feet there were dozens of little heart-shaped fragments of shell. It was just like the picture I'd drawn.

Breaking the Bonds of Karma

One thing I've come to understand over the years is that emotional states eventually become physical. Stress, fear, hurt and loss sink deep into the cells and write their names there. Unattended, they fester and multiply, dividing and reproducing like a shadow DNA. Long after an emotional event has been forgotten, its residue can surface in physical symptoms and deadly disease.

This is why it is so important to experience and process emotions at the time they occur rather than ignoring them and stuffing them down. Tools like the expressive arts are ideal for this, and I am ever grateful for the gift of the CJEA training. But even with the healthy expression of feelings through art and journaling, body and energy work are equally important in completely releasing the effects of emotional trauma.

So it was with real interest and expectation that I took the next step in my healing journey. Once again, the AZHCC proved to be an amazing source of the right contacts at the right time for me. I first met Sherry Anshara while working on the Chamber's Internet radio program. Sherry specialized in cellular release, a form of energy work which enables one to release the cellular memorization of past traumas and dramas.[52] When I learned she would be teaching the process in a workshop during the summer of 2006, I immediately signed up.

The training was intriguing and challenging, but it pushed all of my skeptic's buttons. It was undeniably healing as well, and I hadn't come this far on my journey only to give my inner skeptic the upper hand. It was clear to me by this point that there was much more going on in this Universe than meets the eye.

Through a few different techniques—hands at a distance, hands-on, and vocal toning—we partnered up and learned to intuit where in someone's body a memorized trauma was being held. Then energetically we would help them to release it. We did this by focusing on a part of their body where we sensed a blockage, and then having the person recall what was stored there and how old they were when it happened. All the while, we would send energy with our hands or through vocal toning. We also used an affirmation which stated that although the past could not be changed, we now chose to release what didn't serve us.

Even though Sherry had clearly emphasized the fact that we weren't healing each other—that each of us was healing ourselves—I still felt uncomfortable in the role of intuiting and sending energy. I felt like an amateur who might get it all wrong and cause harm rather than healing. The part of me that was always reaching for the next accreditation or certification was feeling extremely uneasy with just diving in and sending energy into someone's body. What if I sent my own stress or dysfunction into them? What if I took theirs into me? Didn't we all need to spend a lot more time learning how to do this properly? The worrier in me was on high alert, but Sherry just kept assuring us that we could do no harm with the process. We were simply channels for a Universal energy that was available to everyone.

Everybody else seemed so much better at it than I felt, and so much more comfortable with the process, too. Most of the students seemed able to literally see the things that Sherry described as "karmic bands" and "strings." These are energetic bonds that keep us trapped and limited into certain sets of experiences, like always being a victim or always experiencing lack. These bands also keep us bound to certain people in dysfunctional ways. Sherry explained that it was like walking around in a suit with a bunch of Velcro straps sticking out of it. Each strap, coded for a specific kind of dysfunction, was just waiting to attach itself to someone with the complimentary connecting piece.

I understood what she was saying in theory, but I didn't *see* a thing. While everyone else exclaimed that they could see it as she pointed out a "band" protruding from someone's leg or tugged a "string" from a torso, I saw nothing but empty air. I felt like shouting, "The emperor has no clothes!"

I couldn't see the bands, but I could absolutely feel the power of the work. As I took my turn to be worked on, I began tapping into deep memories. I could feel a rise in temperature and an almost electrical feeling of energy coursing through my body.

In one powerful experience, I found myself in a very dark place and I felt like I couldn't breathe. My chest felt constricted by some enormous pressure. I felt a deep fear that bordered on terror. Sherry came over to the table I was lying on and helped my partner to talk me through what I was feeling. She asked me where I was and how old I was, but I couldn't figure it out. What eventually occurred to me was that I was in my mother's womb and the fear I was feeling was *her* fear.

I am the baby of my family, born five years after my sister, Christine, who is the last of three stair-step children, each born a year apart. I knew that my mother had been told she shouldn't have any more children after my sister was born. I've never been sure whether that was due to a physical problem or to her mental state. I believe she'd had some kind of nervous breakdown after the first three children came along. She told me that she'd really wanted another child, though, and eventually she'd gotten the doctor to approve of her trying. Apparently she and my dad were both thrilled with my arrival.

What was coming up for me now, though, was her incredible fear as I was being born. The imprint it seemed to leave in me was a feeling that perhaps I had no right to be born at all. Suddenly, my extreme shyness, my self-consciousness and my feelings of alienation and isolation as a child (in spite of the fact that I was totally loved and spoiled rotten as the baby of the family) began to make sense to me. I remembered the session with Dr. Neddermeyer when I'd recalled not being allowed to have a birthday party. What I felt now was that of course I shouldn't celebrate my birthday because I wasn't even supposed to be here. It was the deepest feeling of unworthiness I've ever felt in my life.

Now it may be that my mother never felt that fear at all. Nevertheless, it was a story I had written into my cellular structure. While it's interesting to discover where a feeling like unworthiness came from, it's almost beside the point. We must take ownership of that feeling within us and change it there, despite how and when it formed.

And Sherry was gently telling me that I could now choose to let that story go. It no longer had to pattern my life. As I repeated the words after her, I felt a tremendous release. After that day's energy work, I sweated the whole night long. I felt nauseated and exhausted for days. Sherry assured me that was a sign of releasing unhealthy memories from my body and suggested Epsom salt baths to further support the release that was occurring.

One of Sherry's main messages throughout the training was that we need to examine our belief systems. She asked us to look at the first letter of each word in the phrase, "Belief System," and to realize that that's just what most of them were: B.S. For all those things we "know" are true, we need to ask, "*Who says so?*" and "*Is it really the case?*" Many of our belief systems are totally inaccurate, but they shape and form our every experience.

This experience I'd internalized of having no right to be born is probably so far from the truth and reality of what my mother actually felt that she'd not even have a clue what I was talking about if I tried to explain it to her. But regardless of what actually transpired at my birth, somehow I'd taken on this belief system of unworthiness as early as that, long before the nuns at school had a chance to reinforce it. That was something I had been consciously unaware of until this exploration of cellular memory.

We incarnate with infinite potential and a clean slate (unless we've chosen to bring karma along), but as we grow we take on all these beliefs that limit us. Sherry insisted that we didn't have to do that. If we had taken on false beliefs, we could now choose to release them at this deepest, physical level so that they would no longer limit our lives.

As for karma, Sherry explained that it was a game we didn't have to play. It was just a deeper form of cellular memorization that we were in the habit of bringing forward into each new life. But we didn't *have* to. She drew a sideways eight on her flipchart and asked us if we knew the meaning of that symbol.

"Infinity!" most of us shouted.

"Bullshit!" was her reply.

As she drew over the symbol with her black marker, going around and around it again, she explained that it represented a closed loop of energy. Stagnation. Stuckness. It represented karma and the endless loop we've bought into as a given, when it really is a choice. We can choose to let go of whatever patterns and power struggles we may have been locked into for lifetime after lifetime.

There is no Power out there that demands we pay for whatever sins we may have committed in a past life. There is no demand for a balancing of the scales. We can choose to let go of the past. We can simply release the unhealthy patterns and memories. We don't have to play. She drew another symbol, a spiral, and said that was a better symbol for eternity, a continuous spiral of growth.

The images stuck with me as I went into my next treatment. As my partner put her hands beneath my head and channeled energy through my body, I thought of Cameron and whatever karmic crap had bound us into this destructive, painful cycle. I saw myself with a big pair of scissors, cutting that black sideways eight at the center, splitting it into two perfect circles that could spin out unfettered into beautiful spirals of light. I wanted to free Cameron and myself to be able to do our own work without the entanglement, without the prison of karma. My only regret would be if that meant severing the bond of love.

I spoke to Cameron from my heart. I told him that I loved him. I told him that someday I wanted to be together again, but only if we could do that without the drama. If he wanted to come back into a future life with me, we had to leave the karmic baggage at the gate.

Whatever pain we may have caused each other, we needed to let go of it now. I was done with it and I wouldn't play anymore. I made a choice in the deepest layer of my being to break the bonds of karma, keeping only love.

Egypt Calls

Just before I began exploring cellular release, an email invitation arrived in my inbox which would eventually take my healing journey to a whole new level. To a whole new continent, for that matter!

John and Carmen LaMarca, publishers of the WholeLife Pages,[53] a holistic directory in which I advertised, were putting together a trip to Egypt. The first twelve advertisers to commit to the trip would be featured speakers on a Nile River cruise and could get their trip for free. I didn't hesitate for a fraction of a second. My finger hit the reply button faster than my brain could even process the thought.

"Absolutely! Sign me up," I typed, then hit the send button before any voice of caution could take the wind out of my sails. Egypt! How awesome that would be! It held the allure of ancient mysteries. I'd never imagined actually going there. It wasn't the kind of travel my husband and I would normally consider. But suddenly the thought of seeing the pyramids or gazing up at the enigmatic and ancient face of the Sphinx filled me with longing and wonder. A Nile River cruise! Imagine that! The opportunity to be a speaker was inviting, as well, because I knew it would be great exposure for my coaching practice.

I had no idea when the trip was scheduled, what the details of the itinerary were or exactly what I had to do to travel for free. I'm not sure I've ever been so quick to commit to something so big with so little information. Until the moment that email arrived, I hadn't even known how badly I wanted to go. Suddenly I was filled with wanderlust. I was going to Egypt!

A few minutes after sending the email, I called David on his cell phone. "Hey honey, how would you like to come with me to Egypt on a Nile River cruise?" I asked excitedly.

After an uncomfortably long silence on the other end of the line, David finally said, "Uh, not really."

"But I can go for free," I said, my heart sinking.

"Why?"

"Because I'll be a speaker on the cruise," I explained.

"But why Egypt?" he wanted to know.

"Why Egypt?! It would be awesome to see Egypt! Wouldn't you love to see the pyramids? WholeLife Pages is putting this trip together and twelve of their advertisers can go for free. I think it would be amazing."

"Huh. Well, let me put some thought into it and I'll talk to you later."

I was extremely disappointed with David's reaction, but rather than taking the wind out of my sails, it seemed to strengthen my resolve. I was going to Egypt whether David wanted to or not. I would go by myself if I had to.

Before David got home from work that day, I did a little research on the trip, finding more information by following the links in the email that had been sent. The trip would begin in late February 2007. In order to travel for free, I'd have to book five paying passengers. Our group of 75 to 100 travelers would have the cruise ship to ourselves and the presentations would be made while we cruised the Nile between ports. The itinerary included the Pyramids, the Sphinx, a private visit to the Cairo Museum and many temple sites including Luxor. I figured it wouldn't be too hard to book five people. Who wouldn't want to go to Egypt?

When David got home and I explained the whole thing to him, he agreed to come with me, not because he had any real interest in Egypt, but because he wanted to support me in the business opportunity it represented. Being able to speak on the cruise could bring me connections and help me to build my coaching clientele. I didn't care what his reasons were. I had my first paying passenger!

Next I spoke to several of my friends. Trish wanted to go for sure and a few weeks later her mother also expressed an interest. Only two more to go! I sent out a blast email to everyone on my mailing list and added information about the trip to my website.

David paid his travel fee in full and Trish and her mother each made a deposit to hold their space.

I decided to do a Visioning® collage about the trip to Egypt to solidify the reality of it in my mind. I didn't have too many magazines in my stash with pictures of Egypt, but I did find an old National Geographic with photos of some of the artifacts from King Tut's tomb and I was able to find some photos of the Sphinx and Great Pyramid on the Internet.

I had not quite finished the collage when I became very ill, a victim of a salmonella infected salad mix. I'd glued some of the images down and was sorting through a pile of cut-out pictures when I began to feel feverish and nauseated. While I spent several days in bed weathering out the effects, my new kitten, Scooby, had a field day with the images I'd cut out and left loose on the table. By the time I was able to come back to finish my Egyptian vision, most of the pictures had been ripped to shreds, including a few that I had already glued down. I finished placing and gluing what I could salvage, but the finished collage just didn't speak to me the way others had in the past. Maybe I still wasn't feeling too well. Or maybe Scooby knew something I didn't.

I hadn't heard much from John and Carmen about who the other speakers were or how they were coming along with their bookings. By September, I was still trying to book my last two travelers. I was beginning to worry that I wouldn't be able to pull it off. Then I learned that no one else had booked a single passenger! Because all of the deposits were due on the hotels and the cruise ship and only my three travelers had sent in any money, the trip had to be canceled. I was devastated.

The travel arrangements were being handled by Sheila Reed, the owner of Luminati Egyptian Travel.[54] Sheila, like John and Carmen, was a member of the AZHCC and I'd had an opportunity to tell her how excited I was about going to Egypt at one of our luncheons. When she spoke to me about having to cancel the WholeLife trip, she mentioned that she was taking a small group to Egypt in November, three months earlier than the trip I'd been planning to take. If my friends and I wanted to go on that trip and I could book two more people, she'd still let me travel for free.

Unfortunately, the new time frame would not work for Trish and her mother as both of them were moving into new homes in November. David, who'd only been interested in going to support me in my business, no longer wanted to go if I wouldn't be making a presentation, especially if it meant paying for both of us. But since he'd already paid his trip in full, he said I could just go on my own if Sheila could transfer his funds to cover my trip. I called Sheila and told her to book me for November.

Later as I looked at my Egypt collage I chuckled when I realized that the central image, the one that traditionally represents the self, was a woman in a caftan walking alone across a sand dune. Although the planned trip was to have been with a large group, I'd subconsciously visioned a different sort of trip, a solitary trip, and that was exactly how it was going to play out.

Egypt Calls

I *would* be traveling alone in the sense that my husband and friends would not be with me. Our group would be small, only six of us including Sheila, rather than a large group of up to 100. The itinerary for this trip would be nearly identical to what had been planned for the WholeLife trip as far as the sites we would visit, but the theme would be completely different.

Besides running her Egyptian travel business, Sheila is a channel. She's been channeling an entity by the name of Menita Ishmil since 1986. Once a year she makes a special trip to Egypt during which Menita calls the shots. He determines the theme for the journey and guides ceremonies at the sacred sites. She believes he even attracts the particular travelers that end up taking these special journeys.

Menita had specified that this trip would be about exploring "Our Ancient Oneness." We would be looking at past lives and connecting to lives we'd all lived in Egypt long ago. We would also do work at each sacred site to open our chakras. At some point during the journey, we'd each have an opportunity for a private channeling session with Menita.

On many levels, the November trip sounded even more appealing than the free trip had. I had a feeling that it could be a deeply healing journey.

The theme of past lives captured my attention right away, and chakra work was something I felt I needed. The personal power issue that had come up in my regression work and the stuck feelings I constantly struggled with seemed to me to be chakra blockages. Body dialogue work that I'd done in the past kept pointing out problems in my throat chakra, the chakra that relates to finding and claiming one's voice. The idea of channeling was intriguing and I wondered what Menita might have to say to me.

I was beginning to get the feeling that once again someone or something was orchestrating things for my benefit. Had that original email arrived in my inbox advertising this specific trip, along with its substantial price tag, rather than the WholeLife free trip, I would have wistfully thought, "That would be cool, but I can't afford it." Instead of pressing reply, I would have hit the delete key without a second thought. It was only that initial possibility of traveling for free that had allowed me to jump at the opportunity. By the time the first trip had fallen through, I was already halfway to Egypt in my mind. By that time, there was nothing that could have stopped me from going.

A Taste of Things to Come

In the months before my trip to Egypt, I was hosting the AZHCC's Internet radio program fairly regularly, interviewing some very interesting guests.[55] Achieve Radio headquarters, where the show was recorded, is located in an eclectic little shopping district in downtown Glendale.[56] I'd driven there many times, parked, and walked by the storefronts on my way to the studio.

Right down the street from the studio was an astrology shop. On my last hosting engagement before leaving for Egypt, I noticed a large display of Egyptian artifacts in their front window. Had those been there all along and I just now noticed them? Or was this a new display? Intrigued, I decided I would stop in and check it out after the radio show was over.

During a commercial break in the live-broadcast show, another AZHCC acquaintance of mine, Sherri Devereau, stepped into the studio. She had just written a book about her experiences as a psychic EMT[57] and was soon going to have her own radio program, so she'd stopped in to talk to the station manager. In the few minutes we had to chat, she mentioned that she was doing readings down the street at the astrology shop and that I should stop by after the show. I felt the familiar goosebumps of synchronicity in the works.

After the broadcast, I visited the astrology shop and looked for Sherri. I found her tarot reading table set up directly below the Egyptian display. Coincidence? I thought not.

I intuitively understood, as I stood looking at Sherri seated beneath the Egyptian display, that the Universe was shouting, "Pay attention!"

I sat down to have a reading and she had me select from several decks of tarot cards. I picked a non-standard deck with illustrations that intrigued me. Sherri laid out the cards and proceeded to tell me many things about my past, present and future.

Two of the cards she turned for my past were "Integration" and "Sorrow." She said that I'd done a good job of integrating my yin and yang, my shadow selves and my life experiences. In addition, while I'd experienced great sorrow, I'd been able to move past it. That seemed to summarize the work of the past two years of my life.

One of the most intriguing things came from one of the three cards she turned up for my present: "Karma," turned upside-down. She interpreted this to mean that I'd done a good job of resolving my karma and that I had little left to work through. I thought that was extremely interesting in light of my recent cutting of the bonds during the cellular release work. It also seemed to make sense of all the trouble I'd had whenever I tried to do a past life regression. Maybe there was just nothing there I needed to know.

Two of my future cards were "Burden Carrier" and "Beyond Illusion." Sherri had me take a close look at the burden carrier. It was a shrunken, bent person carrying a larger person on his back up a steep incline.

She said, "This is not who you want to be. It's time to release the burdens, especially other people's burdens. Stop carrying them. Clear out any stored burdens and be done with them."

I thought of all the years I'd carried Cameron's pain in my own soul, all the years I'd worried and felt responsible for him. When he'd died, I'd asked Dr. Capacchione, "What can I do to keep the void he's left from being filled with more drama and more codependence?" Her answer had been that I needed to turn all that compassion and concern inward and heal my own Inner Child.

I felt that I'd been doing that, and yet there was the growing responsibility, shared with my siblings, of becoming caretaker for my aging parents. It was often emotionally draining and there was the potential there for becoming bent and broken like the image in the card. I would never turn my back on my parents, but I didn't want to *carry* them on my back either. I could see I must find a way to care for them without taking on their problems as my own. I would need to steer clear of all the worry and fear that had filled my relationship with Cameron and find a healthier way of being helpful.

The "Beyond Illusion" card promised answers. Sherri said it meant that soon all would be clear. It would all make sense. She felt it was a near-term future, within three months. I hoped that it was true, that I would find something I needed on this trip so that I finally *could* make sense of it all. I fervently hoped I was not setting too much stock in the power of this trip. It just seemed to me that maybe Egypt held the key to everything.

After the basic life reading, Sherri asked me if I had a specific question. I asked about Egypt. I asked if it would be all I hoped it would be, if it would bring me healing and if there was anything in particular that I should watch for. Three of the cards she turned were "Birth," "The Mother," and "The Beast."

"Birth" signified a brand new experience, a new birth, a new beginning. Sherri felt "The Mother" had to do with a mother energy connection I would make, perhaps with one of the Egyptian goddesses. I wondered, too, if it might not represent a resolution of my own mother energy, a new way of looking at my relationship to Cameron and a new level of closure.

Sherri's take on "The Beast" was that I needed to be careful not to get caught up in the rush of the trip and thereby miss the most important parts. She warned me not to be so focused on the next stop on the itinerary that I missed what was right in front of me in the now. That made sense, and on the trip I took her advice, but later I would begin to see another meaning for that card.

The Trip that Was Meant to Be

Finally, the day arrived when my Egyptian journey would begin. On November 4, 2006, I flew from Phoenix to New York and the next day I would fly to Cairo. I could hardly believe I was on my way.

The in-flight movie on the plane from Phoenix to JFK was *Broken Bridges*.[58] It was a story about love, loss, death and dysfunctional families making amends. Dixie, the young girl in the movie played by Lindsey Haun, writes and sings *Broken,* a song about the inner beauty and strength that can arise from the breaking of one's heart.[59]

I had Cameron on my mind, as the movie was about losing a son and a brother, as well as trying to heal the wounds between a parent and a child. It seemed like Cameron was talking to me again. It seemed he was trying to show me it was never too late to put things right and never too late to heal. It gave me a good feeling about the journey ahead of me. It seemed to confirm my intuition that this trip would bring a new level of healing and closure to my life.

Before I left home I had considered bringing some of his ashes with me on this journey. I thought I might create some closure by ceremoniously scattering a part of his ashes somewhere in Egypt, the land of mummies and immortality. I thought, too, that in a way I would be bringing him with me. I thought that maybe we could find closure and healing *together*.

But I couldn't figure out what kind of container to use to hold the ashes. I wondered if you needed special permission to transport human remains or if they'd take the ashes away from me at customs. When it came right down to it, I just couldn't open that little sealed cardboard box and be confronted with the sight of what it contained.

At that moment, I'd felt Cameron's presence and he seemed to tell me, "I *will* be there with you, Mom. You don't need ashes for that!" I'd gone into my office and picked up that little black heart

The Trip that was Meant to Be

shell, the first one he'd given me at South Padre. I'd just held it for a minute and reabsorbed the knowledge that he would *always* with me and that love never dies.

~~~

When we deplaned at J.F.K., there was a big plasma screen TV in the terminal showing a short film of Egypt that included views of the Pyramids, the Sphinx and people riding camels. It was a nice synchronicity that felt like an early welcome to Egypt, even thought I was still in the U.S.

Sheila and I had come in on the same plane and we stayed overnight at the same hotel in New York. The rest of our group would be meeting us in Cairo the next day. We had dinner together, and she explained to me a little bit about Menita, the entity she channels, and how he sets up these trips. He tells her when to go and what the agenda will be. It is always a surprise to her. There's a kind of magic in the way the trips come together and the people end up being just right.

She said, "He's never done anything with past lives before and I'm a little perplexed by it. He's usually so much about the here and now, about being in the present. I'm a little put off by it, to tell you the truth, but I've learned to just follow his lead."

That surprised me. I had assumed the past life work was old hat, standard procedure for these Menita trips. I was amazed to learn that it wasn't.

"I think it's for me," I said with dawning wonder. "The past life stuff, I mean."

I told her about losing Cameron and how I always thought there must be a boatload of karma between us. I told her how every time I'd tried to do past life regressions all kinds of blocks and barriers came up. I told her about Sherri's tarot reading and the upside-down karma card. I told her I thought the free trip was a setup and that the Universe wanted me to end up on *this* trip. I was becoming more certain by the minute that this trip was meant to be.

Maybe Menita would be able to shed some light on whatever history Cameron and I shared. Maybe the chakra work at the temple sites would help me break through my blockages. Maybe I'd find the answers and see things clearly as the tarot cards had said. Maybe at last all the pieces would fall into place.

Lizards and Fishes

I'd been reading *Dreams of Isis,* by Normandi Ellis, in preparation for my journey. I was about halfway through it and I'd already marked many passages that moved me or made me think. Ellis had found such deep meaning and healing in her Egyptian journeys and studies that I could only hope I might find the same. I'd brought the book with me to finish on the trip.

I laughed out loud when I read her description of the scarab beetle as the Egyptian symbol for transformation. The humble dung beetle, laying its eggs in a big ball of shit, brings forth new life from the dark and smelly excrement. "Not only does Shit Happen," she wrote, "but Shit Transforms."[60]

It reminded me of the time, early in our marriage, that David had told me about tumblebugs and I'd thought *he* was full of shit! I'd seen some kind of big beetle and he'd told me it was a tumblebug. He was always taking advantage of my gullibility and I was sure that's what he was doing this time. I just could not believe there was such a thing as a beetle that spent its days rolling around a big ball of cow dung. He told me to look it up in the dictionary and I was much chagrined to find that he was right.

Now, after all the shit we'd been through together, I'd come across the same story in ancient form. The ancient Egyptians saw Kheperi, the scarab, as a god. After the sun's nightly journey through the Underworld, it was Kheperi who pushed the sun back up into the sky each morning.[61] Shit happens and then Kheperi rebirths it as light. Alchemy happens in the dark, smelly, undesirable places. Just like the song had suggested in the in-flight movie, *Broken Bridges*, it's the dark places that shape who we become.

Ellis wrote that there was a statue of the scarab at Karnak. Anyone who walked around the statue nine times in prayer would receive the blessing of "the Ennead," the sacred number nine—completion, conclusion, manifestation.[62] I wondered if that would be where I would finally find closure.

A few weeks before, I'd had a dream of lizards that seemed to carry a similar theme of transforming the darkness into light.

October 11, 2006 — Lizards

There are several small rooms, more like alcoves. Each alcove has an arched doorway. I am preparing these rooms for the arrival of others. I hang a lizard's tail at each doorway. As I do so, hundreds of lizards come up from the sea as if to pay homage — to me, or to the alcoves, or to the process this represents.

Upon awakening, I thought the dream might be introducing me to a new totem animal. Totem animals, or animal guides, come to lend us their unique powers and traits, or to ask us to find and exercise those traits within ourselves. At various times, totem animals had come to me in my dreams to guide me through the next stage of my life. The bear had come to me long ago when I first began to search for my true, authentic self. I had likened that stage of my life to awakening from a long winter's sleep, ravenous for spiritual growth. Next came the turtle, who carried many messages for me: come out of your shell, stick your neck out a bit, slow and steady wins the race. The turtle can also navigate in water or on land, and so seems to bridge the physical and spiritual realms. Turtle is the dreamer in me, and the one whose eyes and ears have been open to receiving messages from Cameron since his passing.

I thought about the qualities of lizards and the first thing that occurred to me was their amazing power of regeneration. If a lizard loses its tail, it grows a new one. I immediately recognized that loss had been the spark for regeneration in my own life, too. If not for the loss of Cameron, I would never have begun this amazing journey that was taking me home to myself. I was beginning to see his death as a true gift, and I was amazed by his generosity.

Living in Arizona and owning cats, I've seen my share of tailless lizards. I've seen the apparent cruelty that cats inflict on the lizards, batting them about and carrying them in their mouths only to drop them and chase them some more. But often the lizard wins the battle. The cat pounces, the lizard loses his tail and then races away to live another day.

The loss of Cameron had felt just like that. It was as though I'd been battered and beaten for years only to finally suffer a sudden and stunning amputation. Yet I'd been hiding out licking my wounds long enough. It was time to take a lesson from the lizard.

The dream was about transformation, the same kind of transformation that the scarab represents. It seemed to be challenging me to grow a new tail. Could I allow the loss to transform me? Could I find a new *tale* to tell about my life and about my loss?

By hanging lizards' tails at the alcove doorways, it seemed I was preparing the way for others to make this same journey of transformation. The hundreds of lizards coming up from the sea seemed to be supporting me or honoring me for this work.

I drew my dream and, using the two-handed dialogue, I spoke to the lizards.

Lizards from the sea, who are you?
We are your source and your destiny.
Why have you come to me now?
You are ready.
What is it you ask of me?
Close the circle
What circle – how do I do that?
The way will be clear
What gift do you bring to me?
Completion

Surely you don't mean completion of my life – the end?

Every ending holds its own beginning and every beginning knows its end

My drawing emphasized the lizards coming up from the sea, and to me they looked like amoebic blobs or fish with feet. It had a primordial, Darwinian feeling to it. I thought of the model of evolution that tells us we all began in the sea and that fish eventually grew feet and ventured out onto dry land where life continued its metamorphosis over and over again through the eons until humankind finally appeared.

As always, the micro mimics the macro. We each go through this same continuous metamorphosis in our own personal lives, being born and reborn, constantly evolving as the events of our lives mold and shape us.

Contemplating my drawing, I played around with words in free association, and then finally composed a rough poem.

> Emergent life, sperm to womb
> Single cell splits into amoebic shapes
> We all begin as fish and grow from there
> Legs emerge and we stand on our own two feet
> We begin in watery safety
> Secluded, cocooned, alone
> Emerging into the great wide world
> We seek connection
> And tremble when it's severed
> Birth, life, death
> The cycle renews itself
> With death opening the door again to birth
> Both for the departed

> And for those left behind
> Their safe stories shattered
> Broken bodies left to grow new tales

Now, here I was in Egypt, a few weeks later, reading Ellis' words as she wrote about the transient nature of physical form and the symbolic meaning of fish in the Egyptian context. The smell of fish could represent death and decay on the one hand, while the fish's watery realm could also represent the beginnings of life in the womb.[63] Fetus and corpse, the beginning and the end, the Alpha and the Omega. The unbroken circle of the snake eating its own tail.

Ellis' wrote that the fish may symbolically represent "the peculiar wisdom acquired before birth or after death—a kind of mystic foreknowledge, as if in the beginning of life, the end were foreshadowed; and simultaneously in the end, the new beginning is revealed."[64] What she wrote was hauntingly similar to what my dream lizards had said about beginnings and endings being intimately intertwined. This convergence of her ideas and my dream dialogue and poetry was intriguing to say the least.

In the past few years I'd had dozens of dreams about fish. Most of the time, I was trying to save them, to take care of them. Often I was searching for them or finding them in odd places, as if I'd put them in storage and then forgotten them there. Always I felt a deep passion for the fish in my dreams and a longing for connection to them. Puzzling out what fish might represent, I'd thought they might be a metaphor for my spiritual nature, since they live their lives immersed in water, which to me is the spiritual realm.

Ellis' imagining of them as the keepers of that larger knowledge we hold in the realm before birth and after death did not contradict my interpretation, but deepened it. It was as though in my dreams of fish I'd been seeking the answers and the clarity that I knew was mine in that other realm, the secret story and purpose of my own incarnation.

In the Big Wave dream I'd had just before Cameron died, the little boy was holding a baggie with a fish in it. Perhaps the boy was holding it out to me not only as a foreshadowing of Cameron's death, but also as the fetal gift of my own new beginning. Perhaps what the little boy held in that bag was the wisdom and the mystery of our coming together and falling apart in this lifetime, the secret agreements we'd made in the time before time.

There was something in all of this that I was meant to remember. Something just beyond my grasp. Cameron had come and gone through my life like a piece of a puzzle, like some kind of clue, as slippery and elusive as a fish in a stream.

Dreaming Egypt

Most nights of my life have been filled with rich, ceaseless dreaming. Often, the memory of those dreams eludes me in the morning. Magical encounters, illuminating ideas, healing ceremonies and harrowing initiations have filled the night only to be swept away by the dawn, leaving nothing but ephemeral fragments and impressions. At other times, I may recall the stories that unfolded in the night and know them to be full of meaning, but find that meaning to be just out of my grasp in waking hours.

Once I dreamed that I stood over an architect's table and laid out before me were the blueprints of the Universe. In my dream, I suddenly understood how it all worked. Everything made sense and everything held such beauty it took my breath away. In the morning, I couldn't recall what it was that I had known so clearly in my dream, but some part of me still held the awe and reverence for the perfection of it all.

Over the years I've come to understand that it doesn't always matter whether the dream is recalled or understood. The magic, the learning, the healing, the initiation still takes place. The knowledge of it may be left in the dreamspace, but the effects are still felt in waking life.

Egypt was that kind of dream for me.

Despite journaling about my experiences while I was there and taking hundreds of photographs, it was like walking through a dream. Fragments of the dream stand out for me, like sparkling shards of light from a many-faceted diamond—a diamond so large that I can't see the whole thing with my waking eyes.

Turn the gem this way and I'm standing dwarfed and humbled at the feet of the Sphinx, knowing that it knows much more than I know. The stone shifts and I'm lying in pitch darkness, bathed in sound, inside an ancient sarcophagus in the heart of the Great Pyramid, sensing life in the darkness beyond me and my fellow sojourners. Another flash of the diamond and I'm seeing

Cameron's face perfectly reflected in the dark complexion, full lips and deep brown eyes of some young Egyptian man and knowing this sacred land of Egypt has been home to him many times. Another angle finds me experiencing powerful electrical surges throughout my body as I connect to the ancient and mysterious energy of this magical place.

In Egypt, mysteries were revealed, answers were given and meaning was found. In a handful of crystalline moments, I found total peace in the core of my being. It was as if once again I stood before that architect's desk and knew the perfection of everything.

In dark, ancient spaces filled with the living energy of Egyptian gods and goddesses, alchemy took place within me. The effects of that alchemy are still bubbling up, for it took place in the part of me that lives in dreams. As time passes, the change that was wrought continues to percolate into my waking world. Glimmers of the truths Egypt granted me reveal themselves slowly and gently as I become ready to accept them into consciousness.

As the Wiz Kid said in the Big Wave dialogues, "Wisdom in small doses. Only what can be handled at any given time."

What follows, then, is like a dream half-remembered. I can relate only the parts of the journey that I clearly recall. And I *choose* to relate only those experiences which make sense to me and which I know were profoundly healing. I know that, like a dream, this journey carries many layers of meaning for me and I will continue to decipher its messages for years to come. While I did my best to journal at the end of each day, we often visited several sites within a single day and what I saw and felt at each place sometimes became jumbled in my mind. In addition, I wandered through most of Egypt in an altered state, which makes it difficult to be clear about everything. So, it may be that I've gotten some of the "facts" turned around, but what I tell you next is nothing but the truth.

Meeting Menita

Menita first appeared to us on the bus as we were on our way to the Step Pyramid at Saqqara. The physiological changes in Sheila as Menita stepped into her body were amazing. Her honey-brown eyes became piercing black coals. Her body mass seemed to shift, becoming harder somehow and more forceful. The voice that came through was deep and masculine, with a pattern of speech quite different from Sheila's own. Menita had a wry sense of humor and seemed to carry an ancient wisdom that he was ready to impart only to those who would take him seriously. There was no doubt in my mind that someone else was present in the space Sheila's body occupied.

In the first moments in which he came into our presence, Menita turned to me. "We have much to talk about, you and I," he said, and I felt his black eyes were looking clear through me and deep into my soul.

He then turned to the group at large and began to lay out our agenda for the day. He posed the following question: "We are approaching an ancient space in an ancient land and you have all been here before. What would it mean to walk through this moment in the very footsteps you once walked before? Indeed, how could you do any less?"

The entrance to Saqqara is a corridor between two long lines of columns. Menita challenged us to feel time and sound within the space the columns created. We were asked to see and feel the columns as music, solidified. Within a darkened niche, we were invited to tone: a humming kind of vocalization which, if done right, can set the whole body to vibrating. My tones were tentative and searching. I settled in at a middle ground note, sounded out in a timid "Ooooooh," while the voices of the others rose and fell around me. I didn't feel the spirit of it, I guess. Maybe I just needed to warm up to it.

Menita said to the group, "Good. You've found your sound," and when he said it, I felt powerful. But when it came time to sound my tone with confidence, I felt weak and lame.

Saqqara, according to Menita, is a fifth (throat) chakra space. The idea was to open the fifth chakra in order to bring out our voices at the beginning of this journey. It was also a space that would help us to move the desire of the heart up through the fifth chakra and out through the crown to bring about its manifestation. In order to obtain the desire of the heart, one must first be able to speak it. In the beginning was the Word, and it is the Word that speaks all creation into being.

Menita took each of us, one by one, into a little chamber and toned for us while we placed our hands on the stone walls and soaked up the energy of the space and the sound. After he toned for me, he asked me to focus on the desire of my heart so he could help move the energy up. I just felt confused and empty. *What is the desire of my heart,* I wondered? *What is it?* There may have been a time when I thought I knew, but at that moment I hadn't a clue.

Apparently Menita had picked up on my confusion, for he commented at the end of our session, "It happens sometimes. It's because your heart isn't open. Sometimes the heart closes down to protect itself."

Earlier in the year, at a CJEA intensive, I'd collaged a story of the light and the dark. A Buddha image stood at the center of the piece in balance and equanimity, undisturbed by anything around him. In dialogue, I had spoken with the Buddha image and one of the things I had asked was this: *"I see that the chakra energy I've drawn flowing through you stops at the chest. What's that about?"*

The Buddha image had replied, *"It's where you are now. A rest stop at the heart. Soon you will claim your voice."*

Meeting Menita

The heart is the fourth chakra, one step before the fifth, which is voice. A rest stop at the heart, the Buddha had said. All this grief and death and pain, I thought, was like the work I needed to do, an opening of the heart that had to happen before I could get to the voice—to *my* voice.

I hadn't thought of it as *rest*; I'd felt it as stuckness. After the Buddha spoke, I recognized that it was rest in a way. I had needed to honor the space that my loss had opened and give it time to germinate and blossom in my heart before I could find my voice. My heart had been wide open once, and it had been shattered. It seemed only natural that it would be hesitant to risk such vulnerability again. That clay sculpture of my broken heart had told me months ago that it needed time to heal.

Now Menita had recognized this same blockage in me. My heart was still closed and turned inward protecting itself from any more pain. I began to cry in frustration, feeling that perhaps I'd come all the way to Egypt in vain. Perhaps with a closed heart, I would not be able to heal. Menita laughed and said, "We'll work on that. It will change."

One of the amazingly detailed reliefs carved into the walls at Saqqara told the story of three men drowned in a river. It showed the grieving family at the funeral service. Our Egyptologist guide pointed out to us the beautifully captured poignancy of the scene of a distraught woman fallen to the ground, others gathered around her trying to support her. The pain on the woman's face was intimately familiar to me, and I was at once back in the moment when the jail death detectives had come to tell me Cameron was gone. The ancientness of the space reminded me that the story of my own grief was universal and timeless. It was not a story I had to live alone. It was a story we all live as humans.

I went to sleep that night incubating a dream about sound and voice, willing my heart to open. I'm not sure I was even asleep yet, when I had this vision.

> ### *November 7, 2006 — Music*
>
>
>
> *A figure at the top of a stone staircase or the end of a stone hall like that at Saqqara says, "A bit repetitive, this one—hah!" I think it must be Menita who's spoken. I feel a little insulted, but his tone is light, as if in fun. Next, a procession of figures and voices rise and fall through my consciousness. They speak, some of them, a word, a phrase. Their voices flow through me like music.*

I had other dreams in the night, not clearly recalled, but there was something about building over it in layers. Upon awakening it struck me as a message about relating the way the pyramids are built to my loss and to all my experiences. It was as if I was being called upon to build over it all, layer upon layer. Building life and soul and being over the totality of my experience, one layer at a time, each layer smaller and lighter than the last, each layer containing less and less substance, until the peak of the pyramid disappears into the sky. The heaviness of the past transformed into the lightness of air.

Desires of the Heart

After we boarded the Moon Goddess, our home for the Nile cruise portion of the journey, Sheila prepared us for the visit we would make in the morning to the Temple of Isis on the island of Philae.

"Isis is the mother goddess and her temple at Philae is a root chakra site," Sheila explained. "It's a place to release the fears that hold you back and to raise the energy up through you so that you can birth, or manifest, the desires of your heart."

She asked us to spend time before our visit to Philae to form an intention that we could hold clearly in our minds when we arrived there in the morning. She told us we could bring an object, if we wished, for the morning's ceremony, so that it could be imbued with Isis energy, mother energy.

I thought I'd bring the locket that Sarah had given me for Mother's Day right after Cameron died. It held photos of my three children as babies. I wanted to celebrate my own mother energy by having Isis bless this locket, a record of what I'd manifested in flesh and blood and bone: my children, here and gone. I wanted the ceremony to bring blessings to them all. I wanted to acknowledge the universal and eternal bonds of love.

I still felt puzzled about my intention, though. What did I want to manifest? That evening I journaled.

> *What is the desire of my heart?*
>
> *To release blockages.*
>
> *To release fears.*
>
> *To step into my power.*
>
> *Power is a tricky word, though. I don't want angry, violent power. I don't want bitchy power. Not so much judgment. I want calm, still power. The power of presence. The power of love, compassion. The power of right—not being right, as in winning an argument, but right being, as in*

> *standing in my own truth despite any external crap.*
>
> *What is the desire of my heart?*
>
> *Clarity? Wisdom?*
>
> *It's like I can't even focus on form anymore. I don't know what work I want to do, what things I want to have. There are some places I want to see. I want to have what I need. I want to step into the world, to make a difference. But I don't know what that amounts to—how to frame it as an intention. Couldn't Isis simply know my heart?*

On the early morning bus ride to the dock from which we'd be ferried over to Philae, Menita made another appearance. He spoke to us about past lives and explained that every life we've lived in what we call the past and every life we'd ever live in what we call the future were all happening in the same moment. This moment. Now. He explained that our human brains were not equipped to let us feel that. Our current physical form was wired into *this* experience of now, but our core being, the Lord God of our Being, was aware of all of our simultaneous existences. The experiences of every one of our incarnated selves wove through the lives of all the others. Whenever one facet of our being, one physical manifestation of the self, made a breakthrough or attained the next level of enlightenment, the effects rippled through every other incarnation, past and future.

We were the first to arrive on Philae and had the holy of holies in Isis' temple all to ourselves for about twenty minutes. As we entered the chamber, one at a time, Menita gave us each a question to ponder while we were inside. When my turn came to enter, he whispered, "Do you have any idea how beautiful you are? Who are you? It is time to remember."

Once we were all in the chamber, Menita led us in a ceremony of sound. He guided us through a series of tones and vowel sounds meant to pull energy up through our core. The quality of sound in the stone enclosure was powerful and alive. I could feel the vibrations moving through me.

Soon the crowds arrived and the magic of the moment was broken. We began a whirlwind tour of the site, and I felt rushed and pressured. Several large tour groups were being guided around the temple site all at once. As the noise level and the volume of people increased, so did my level of tension. Our Egyptologist guide, Soheila, had a wealth of information about the site, but I felt disconnected and unable to absorb what she was saying. I would have preferred to wander on my own in silence, to spend hours here connecting to the energy of the space itself.

I'd felt pressured the night before, too, when we'd gone to the Nubian market in Aswan. The shops in the bustling open air market were filled to overflowing with exotic wares—spices, oils, carved masks, cloth, musical instruments, jewelry and clothing. Dark-eyed men in long white galabayas beckoned from every open shop front, "Miss. Here. Come here. Very good prices." It reminded me of the beach vendors in Mexico, always promising, "For you today, almost free."

Our guide quickly walked us through the main section of the bazaar, pointing out the "good" shops, where we would be treated honestly and get a fair price. She suggested we stay in pairs or small groups and stick to the shops she had pointed out. She gave us an hour to wander and make whatever purchases we desired.

I felt frustrated. An hour in this marketplace would not be long enough to really enjoy the experience. I knew that our guide's suggestions were well-intentioned, but they felt limiting and restrictive to me. I didn't want to be told where to shop, I wanted to explore. I didn't want to tag along with others into places in which I had no interest.

So I set out on my own and almost immediately felt directionless and disoriented. Not sure what kinds of things I wanted to look at, I was uncertain where to go. I was nervous about the money I was carrying and still a little fuzzy on the conversion factor between dollars and Egyptian pounds. I wasn't sure I'd know the difference between a good price and a rip-off. My Arabic was limited to yes, no and thank you—about the same amount of English as the shopkeepers seemed to know. I felt conspicuously white and female on a dark night in a foreign land.

I began to feel somewhat fearful as the insistent vendors hawked their wares. They seemed more pushy and persistent than the vendors in Mexico. They were less willing to take no for an answer and just let me pass. Some of them would step out in front of me or trail me down the market path.

After I'd wandered for a bit, I wasn't even sure how to get back to our arranged meeting place. I laughed at the surge of relief that flooded through me when I ran into Teryl, another woman from our group, as I entered the next shop. I stuck with her for the rest of the hour and marveled at my contradictory nature. I'd wanted to do things my own way without being herded about, but when left to my own devices I'd felt fearful and lost.

It seemed like a metaphor for my life. When I was feeling controlled or directed by others I wanted freedom, but when I had freedom I felt directionless. It was as if I'd become so used to working under the structure of some externally imposed agenda that I was rudderless without one. I was wandering through the bazaar of life, rich with possibilities, not knowing what I wanted to buy and not knowing the value of the money I carried.

I'd left the corporate world nearly ten years ago to find my own path, and I was still searching. Cameron had been gone over two years now and I was free from all the drama and tension that relationship had created in my life. Sarah and Ryan were grown and taking care of themselves. David generously provided all the financial support and encouragement anyone could ask for. I had all the freedom in the world to be whoever I wanted to be. Why was it so difficult to figure out who that was?

Maybe finding oneself was not so much about *finding* as it was about remembering.

Each of us arrives on this planet almost as a blank slate. Not blank, exactly, but closer to the true core of our "self" than at any other moment in our lives. Immediately we begin to set about accumulating identities, which we mostly do through relationship. We begin to write all our names on that once blank slate:

Worthy (or Unworthy). Loved (or Unloved). Eldest/Youngest. Smart/Stupid. Daughter/Son. Wife/Husband. Mother/Father. Butcher/Baker/Candlestick Maker. We begin to *define* ourselves by the roles we play or the adjectives we or others use to describe us. At times we may erase one name and replace it with another. Our slate is usually so full of names that we think we know who we are. But are any of those names *really* who we are?

For most of my adult life, one of the top names on my list was "Cameron's Mom." When that was erased from my slate, it created a huge void in my accreted identity. Like the lizard that's lost its tail, the erasure of that name left me staring at empty space where there was once living flesh. There is an Egyptian story about this kind of dismemberment.

Isis, the mother goddess in Egyptian lore, was the consort of the first god, Osiris. When Osiris' brother Seth killed him and scattered his dismembered body parts into the Nile, it was Isis who re-membered him by searching for and collecting his scattered parts, piecing them together and then revivifying him. There was only one member missing: his penis, the organ of procreation. This, Isis had to create for herself. Once Osiris, like an ancient Humpty Dumpty, was put back together again, Isis conceived with him their son, Horus. Osiris then became king of the world of the afterlife, while Horus became the new living king, the god who every future pharaoh would embody.[65]

Perhaps the tale of Isis and Osiris was a clue for my own journey. Did I, like Isis, need to find a way to birth something new from my loss and then leave the dead to the afterworld? It seemed to me that the challenge of grief might be just that: to gather together the parts of myself that remained and then birth something new by creating a new self. Or perhaps, as the dream about those ever smaller pyramidal layers had shown, I needed to continue to strip away those accreted identities until all that was left was the truth of me, stripped back down to the core.

What is the desire of my heart? To know who I am.

"Who are you?" Menita had whispered gently. "It is the time to re-member."

Past and Future Lives

About half way through my Egyptian journey, as we cruised the Nile toward Luxor, I met with Menita for a private session. In the quiet seclusion of Sheila's stateroom we sat facing one another across a small table. I watched with fascination as, once more, Sheila's persona was replaced by the more masculine presence of this being she channeled.

"Greetings, Master," the deep and dignified voice began. He called each of us, male or female, "Master," to emphasize that we were each masters of our own being. "There is an entity here with us who is quite intent on having his say. There will be time for that, but first I have much to say to you myself. Hah!"

He began by expanding on the model of past and future lives that he'd first described to us on the way to Philae. "You recall that I said all these lives, these projections of yourself, occur simultaneously, yes? Now, how can that be?"

He grabbed a green, under-ripe date from a bowl of fruit and waved it in front of my eyes. "Here," he said, his black eyes twinkling in merriment, "is your core self, the Lord God of Your Being. Hah!"

He placed the fruit in the center of the table and continued, gesticulating all the while with his hands to illustrate what he said. "Now, imagine a circle that expands out from this center and imagine that circle to be filled with radiating lines, something like the spokes of a wheel. Each of those spokes represents a projection of yourself, an incarnation, a lifetime.

"Here, perhaps," he continued, indicating one of the imaginary spokes, "is a projection which exists, from your perspective in your current lifetime, in what you would call the future, the year 3042, let's say. And here, this other projection, exists in what you call the past. You have many interesting projections, all of them actually in the now, but some past and some future as perceived in your third dimensional illusion of time."

He proceeded to describe several of my past incarnations, most of which quickly became jumbled in my mind: a life in India in a spiritual practice related to Hinduism, another in Rome, another in Atlantis, several in ancient Egypt. I had been an artist, a poet, an oracle, a musician and a writer in various pasts.

As a woman named Maya, I was born to a concubine who protected me from that same fate by teaching me well, nurturing my talents, and then secreting me away to the borderlands between Atlantis and Lemuria, where I learned a special form of hieroglyphics and wrote many books.

In another life, I was an oracle who had two daughters who were also blessed with psychic or intuitive abilities. I was a great mother to them and helped them develop their abilities to the fullest. Menita assured me that these two were with me again in this lifetime and that I knew them now as two dear friends.

"But, in truth, all these lives are simply simultaneous projections emanating from here!" he exclaimed, slapping his open palm down on the date for emphasis. "The idea is to practice walking through *this* moment with the knowing of all these selves so that you can activate the artist, the writer, the oracle, all in the now, by tapping into the *bigger* Now. Hah! The larger Now, where you are all that, where you *are* the I AM. The trick is to know that you are all of these bandwidths at once, to know it so clearly that the whole projection collapses and you return to your core, to the Lord God of your Being."

He jiggled the date for emphasis.

It was a mind-boggling model of how things worked. I could almost grasp what he was saying. It was reminiscent of my thoughts after the dream of finding Cameron drowned in the river and then finding him alive in another part of the river. I'd thought of the multiverse theory then and wondered if Cameron might not be experiencing many other lives that I just couldn't see or imagine. Menita seemed to be saying the same thing and emphasizing the *simultaneity* of it all as well as the interconnectedness. The learning, the gifts, the experiences of all these other "MEs" could be—no, *were*—affecting and informing my "current" existence. And my "current" experience must be affecting all these other "MEs," too. I wondered what kind of a shockwave Cameron's death, and my reaction to it, might have sent rippling through my personal multiverse.

Menita assured me that I had been incarnated in both male and female form many, many times. In one of my male incarnations, I was born in Meso-America in the late 1500s. I was a strong, muscled man with dark skin and beautiful hair. The people in my tribe lived hard and dangerous lives. Growing up to be a strong man was paramount to survival.

In that lifetime, I had a son who was soft and sensitive and I was very hard on him, for I wanted him to grow into a strong and powerful man like me, a brave hunter, a good fighter. My son was not interested in the things I wanted to teach him and as the years went by I became very frustrated. At last, in exasperation, I sent my son away on a trek, alone, imagining that he would have to learn the skills of survival this way. I sent him to a high mountain and bade him not to return without proof that he'd been to the top.

On his journey, he fell and injured his leg badly. Alone and scared, with no one to help him, he died in pain and fear. I waited and waited for his return, but he never came back. When I learned of his death from travelers who'd stumbled upon his remains, I felt extremely guilty and depressed. I had only loved him and wanted him to be strong.

It was such a painful loss that I'd never really lived from that day on. Even when I died in that lifetime, I carried the pain of that loss with me to the other side and vowed not to return to incarnated form for a long, long time. I joined a soul group in another dimension. It was a learning group and I stayed with them for a very long time as Earth counts the years.

At last I felt ready to return. The son from that last tragic lifetime chose to return as well. He wanted to learn why I hadn't loved him. He carried much anger and bitterness and even wanted revenge to some extent.

But all I had for him was love—then and now. In this life, he was once again my son and I was his loving mother. At the end of this lifetime, he finally understood that I had *always* loved him.

Past and Future Lives

"And where he is now," Menita said, "he understands that even more clearly. There is no score to settle. All is well. In 2098, you will have another lifetime together as great friends with no family ties, no grief and no drama."

Suddenly I could see why I'd always feared losing Cameron and carried such a deep sadness in me. I was reliving the loss I'd already (and simultaneously) experienced in Meso-America. Did that "past" life inform this one? Or did this life inform the other? In that other life, Menita had said I never really lived the rest of my life, and I had chosen not to live another life for a very long time. Perhaps I could make a different choice this time: the choice to live fully. Maybe this life was offering me—all of the "MEs"—a chance to heal.

As Menita had been telling the story of my Meso-American incarnation, Cameron had apparently been very present. Menita kept tossing his head and looking over his shoulder as if to shake someone off. At one point, he'd turned and waved his hand into the space behind his head and gruffly said, "Stop poking! In a moment you shall have your chance."

Once the story had been told, Menita finally allowed Cameron to have his say. What Cameron wanted me to know was that I'd been the best Mom, that he loved me so much, that he knew how much I loved him, how much I'd always loved him. He wanted me to know that it was all okay.

Menita then warned me that Cameron loved me so much that he would not move on until I really let him go. He told me it was okay to feel sadness, anger, even some guilt, but only to feel it, to acknowledge the feeling. I should not label it or attach it to any experience or allow my brain to do so. If these feelings arose in me, I should simply say, "I love you, that's all," and let it go.

It seemed to me as though letting go meant making a choice not to continue to identify with past pain. I could almost grasp how releasing my connection to that pain could heal me not only in my current incarnation, but in past and future incarnations as well. If I lived the rest of my life fully and joyfully, then somehow I would be redeeming that Meso-American father, too, and ensuring a future life where Cameron and I could be together as friends with no karmic baggage.

That felt exactly like the decision I'd made when I'd cut the bonds of karma and vowed to hold on to love alone. I did not want to hold Cameron back from his further learning and evolution. It seemed that my guilt and sadness, far from being ways to honor him, were instead ties that bound him. Over the past two years, I had been peeling away the layers of grief and remorse, but now I felt ready to shed the last of it, to set us both free. I so looked forward to that future life where we could be simply the best of friends.

As I left the meeting, my head spinning with all that had been said, I pocketed the under-ripe date that Menita had used in his illustration. I thought of it as the Lord *Date* of my Being, a greenhorn in the great scheme of things. Hah!

Hathor

I felt a strong affinity for the goddess Hathor as soon as we arrived at Dendara, the home of her main temple. She is alternately pictured as a cow with horns holding the sun disk, as a woman with a cow's head, or as a woman with a wide, somewhat triangular human face and the ears of a cow. In this elongated form, the human features of the face are always smiling an enigmatic, Mona Lisa kind of smile. It is a smile of mystery and secrets.

Many powers are attributed to Hathor. She is known as the goddess of joy, dance, celebration and drunkenness.[66] Perhaps I felt so called to her because these were the very things that had been missing from my life recently. Well, not the drunkenness. But my drinking had not been celebratory for a long time. Too often I drank to drown my sorrows. I longed to reclaim joy.

As the goddess of the West, the land of the dead, it is Hathor who welcomes the deceased into the afterlife. She offers the dead protection as they journey through the Underworld.[67] Maybe through her I could connect to Cameron where he was. She is also the goddess of love and, since Cameron had died, it had been becoming clear to me that love was the only thing of true importance in this world. I wanted to embrace everything Hathor stood for.

I felt very connected at Dendara, which is a fourth-chakra, heart energy site. In the sanctuary there, as Menita led us in ceremony, I felt my hands tingle. My feet grew extremely warm, and all at once I felt a rod of energy supporting me from toe to head as we toned Om, Ah and Eh. My heart was full and my head was buzzing.

Unlike the rushed, crowded, noisy experience I'd had at the Temple of Isis, my experience at Dendara felt unhurried and peaceful. It was not that the crowds were any smaller, really, but I had decided at some point after Philae that I would have to carry my own peace and stillness with me despite the rush and the crowds.

I liked this temple a lot and felt quite at home. Hathor's cute little face beamed from atop every column, and I felt her simple joy filter into my very cells.

Near Hathor's temple, I explored the ruins of a dream house. Pilgrims would come to these sanatoriums to seek healing by bathing in sacred waters and then sleeping in small cubicles where they would hope to receive a healing dream.[68] A few thousand years later, more by accident than by design, I was amazed to find myself here in Egypt on that same kind of pilgrimage. It seemed I had been drawn to this place in order to complete my healing journey. As I sat upon the crumbling stone foundation of this dream house, I thanked whatever powers had brought me here.

When we'd visited Philae a few days before, our Egyptologist guide had asked us to ponder the face of Hathor and think about what we saw there. We'd seen her cow-eared, elongated face at the top of several pillars at Philae, where a small temple to Hathor stood in the shadows of the Temple of Isis. Isis and Hathor are something like sisters in ancient Egyptian lore. As time passed, more and more they became interchangeable until they finally merged into Aphrodite, the Greek goddess of love.

The structure of Hathor's face reminded me of the Inuit people, or the Hopi: broad-cheeked, heart-shaped and a little bit Asian. I wasn't sure what our guide was after in asking what her visage evoked in us, but what flashed into my consciousness was the word "rumination." Behind her Mona Lisa smile, she seemed to be pondering the mysteries of the Universe.

Rumination seemed an appropriately cow-like quality: the chewing of the cud and the multiple stages of digestion required by virtue of having many stomachs. I could relate to that. I needed time for rumination. Too much noise and/or information all at once had a tendency to just become a flow of words that slid over and around me without being absorbed or retained. That was why I hadn't been able to take in Soheila's explanations of the hieroglyphs and artifacts at the crowded Temple of Isis. I needed to soak in it in order to soak it in. I needed to chew on things and ruminate until their meanings slowly made themselves known.

Our Egyptologist now pointed out something interesting about Hathor that a past visitor had suggested to her. The shape of Hathor's head and ears was much like a uterus: the face being like a womb, the ears like ovaries and the narrow neck like the birth canal.

Hathor. Goddess of Love. Birther of Life. Love as the animating force of our being. I prayed that she could birth in me that same calm, still peace that I read in her face. I prayed that I could learn to reconnect to and live from love.

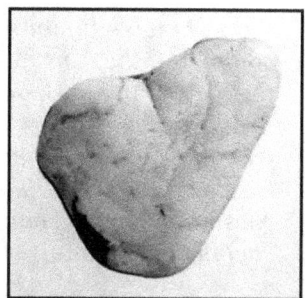

Later that same day we visited Abydos and the temple of Osiris. While Cameron had spoken to me briefly during the session with Menita, it was at Abydos that I received my first physical "hello" gift from him: a beautiful heart-shaped stone lying at my feet on the outer steps of the temple. It was as if, having connected so strongly through the story of our last incarnation together, I was ready now to find his love notes here in Egypt, far from the sea where I'd grown accustomed to finding them.

While I had felt an energetic connection at Dendara, Abydos stimulated my intellectual curiosity. Although it was the most ancient of the sites we visited, the carvings there seemed to represent fantastically modern-looking objects. One lintel in particular displayed what clearly looked liked an airplane, a helicopter, and a battleship. On other walls I saw what looked like giant filament light bulbs, complete with power cords. In one scene, a reptilian looking creature seemed to be gifting the

Egyptians with the secret of electricity. Observing these intriguing scenes, carved thousands of years ago, it seemed to me that what we don't know about our Egyptian ancestors far outweighs what we think we do know. That may be true about most anything we think we understand in life. So maybe Cameron said hello to me there as a nod to the mysteries of the Universe, an acknowledgment of all the unknowns in our own relationship.

When we returned to the Moon Goddess after our tours of Dendara and Abydos, I was exhausted. I went into my cabin to lie down for a few minutes, not intending to sleep, simply to rest. Suddenly, although I did not seem to be sleeping, I found myself dreaming.

November 10, 2006 — Removing the Blockages

I am walking with Sheila (Menita?). Suddenly she begins to cough and she says, "Just a minute." She presses her mouth against the back of my neck and coughs into me as I bend my head forward. I feel this energy tingling through my system, my core, from the bottom of my body upward. After several of Sheila/Menita's coughs, I feel something shift and break in my chest and throat. Then the energy, like an electrical charge, just shoots through me.

The powerfully physical sensation of that electrical surge so startled me that I sat bolt upright in bed. I immediately started to cough violently. I wasn't sure what kind of experience I'd just had. I truly did not feel like I'd fallen asleep. Perhaps rather than a dream, it had been some kind of out of body experience. Somehow I felt certain that the blockages in my heart and throat had finally been cleared away and the energy of the Universe had surged freely through my entire being.

Remembrance

When we arrived at Karnak, I felt an immediate connection to the energy of the space. In the cool stillness of the very early morning, before the sun had risen and well before the crowds would arrive, our small group walked in reverent silence to the Temple of Ramses III, which is dedicated to Amun, the hidden god, the god who permeates and animates all life.

Within the stone walls of the inner sanctuary stood an ancient granite altar where once the statue of Amun would have rested, awaiting the ministrations and prayers of the Pharaoh and his priests. In the eastern wall of this holy of holies, a small window awaited the rising of the sun.

Just outside the sanctuary, Menita helped us to work with sound in order to open up our hearts. He then invited us to circle the altar and I stepped into the space directly facing the window.

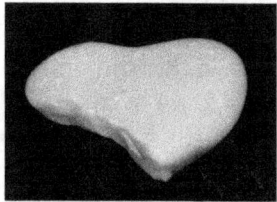

As soon as I had selected my spot, I saw a beautiful white, smooth, heart-shaped stone at my feet. The top of the heart was perfectly formed, but the lower left portion of the heart had a jagged, broken edge—a missing piece.

I felt that Cameron, or maybe the space itself, was saying, *"I understand your pain, the brokenness you have felt in your own heart. I love you. Even though it's been broken, it is perfect still."*

We closed our eyes and raised our voices in sound. The harmony of each of our heart tones melding together was almost celestial. The stone walls around us seemed to feed the sounds back, as if the space were singing along with us. As we toned, the sun rose to an angle that filtered through the eastern window and warmed my face. I turned my head upward, eyes still closed, soaking in the luxuriant light of the dawning day. Spontaneous tears of joy trickled down my cheeks. I felt filled to overflowing with peace and gratitude. As we filtered out of Amun's sanctuary,

Menita told me my heart was finally open and I could feel the truth of his words.

We walked then, again in silence, toward a small temple dedicated to the god Ptah, the architect of the Universe and the creator of all. Perhaps it had been *his* blueprints that I'd studied in that long ago dream.

Ptah's consort, Sekhmet, the lion-headed goddess of personal power, had her own place of honor within his temple. Throughout our journey, Sheila had been promising us that we would be forever changed by our encounter with Sekhmet. She said that once we had stepped into her sanctuary and received her gift of power, we would be able to manifest the deepest desires of our hearts. I had been anticipating this stage of the journey with mixed emotions. I knew that I had been blocked when it came to claiming my own power and I knew that in order to accomplish anything in my life, I needed to accept that I *had* power.

Yet, so many "strong" women seemed to me to always be angry, to get what they wanted by asserting themselves in an overly aggressive way. In politics and in the corporate world, for example, it seemed that the women who "made it" did so by becoming hard and playing a cutthroat game. I didn't want to be a doormat, but something in me recoiled from the sound and fury approach to personal power. My style had always been more diplomatic and compromising. I had to wonder, though, if I sometimes compromised too much and settled for too little.

Sheila's own demonstration of power and presence as we had traveled throughout Egypt had been forceful. Several times, as our Egyptian travel guides handled things in a way not to her liking, she had flashed with anger and argued her point loudly and insistently until she got things done her way. Certainly that had served us, as we were able to get into places not normally open to the public and to enjoy private visits at certain sites. Probably, as a woman dealing with a male dominated Arabic Muslim culture, she would not have gotten very far otherwise. I was grateful that she was our leader, because wherever she went in Egypt, doors opened for her—and therefore for us. Yet, to imagine myself being that assertive made me strangely uncomfortable.

Sekhmet's lioness form seemed to embody that roaring sort of power and, quite frankly, it intimidated me. I had been puzzling over this concept of power ever since the beginning of the trip and wondering what stepping into my own personal power might mean. So it was with an uncertain expectancy that I entered the dark space of Ptah's stone temple.

The space was divided into three small chambers: the central and larger space into which the main door opened and two smaller rooms to the right and left. Upon a stone altar in the central chamber stood what remained of a statue of Ptah, apparently beheaded in an act of vandalism or desecration at some time in the past. The chamber to the left was empty. But to the right we entered a chamber that held a nearly pristine, full-length, larger than life statue of the goddess Sekhmet in all her leonine grace. She took my breath away.

I was unprepared for the beauty, the power and the presence I felt within this holy space. It was a small room, lit only by a narrow slit in the stone ceiling directly above the statue. After we'd all stepped inside Sekhmet's sanctuary, the shrine's attendants closed the chamber's wooden door, leaving us in pitch darkness broken only by the delicately filtered rays of sunlight that bathed the goddess in a heavenly light.

We approached Sekhmet with reverence and awe. When, drawn by some mysterious impulse, I placed my hand above her left breast where her heart would be, the polished black granite statue seemed to radiate the warmth of a living, breathing being. I was in such an altered state by then, that I do not recall what form our ceremony took in this space. I remember Menita gently taking the broken heart stone from my hand and placing it on top of Sekhmet's staff before we all joined hands around her. I felt her presence and power well up in me, and it was a power that came not from anger and ferocity but from such tender gentleness that I was once again moved to tears.

Like Aslan, the god-figure lion in the C. S. Lewis stories, underneath Sekhmet's ferocious exterior, underneath her potential for righteous, roaring anger, I felt nothing but an overwhelming compassion and love. It was the love of a mother for her child, an intimate knowledge and sharing of that child's pain, and a desire to soothe all the hurts that her child had ever experienced.

All at once I was filled with the truth of my own being. It welled up and overflowed, staggering me with its strength. It was a strength that came from stillness and peace and love. Suddenly all the dark places within me were filled with light. I understood in that moment that, just like the narrow crevice in the roof allowed the filtered light to illuminate the goddess, it was the broken places in my heart that would allow my own inner light to shine through.

Now I could see that the breaking of my heart had been Cameron's gift to me, and I was overwhelmed with gratitude. I felt healing and a great opening up through which my tears flowed freely. I am certain that I could never adequately convey the magnitude of this epiphany, for as I struggle to write this now, the immensity of that feeling rises in me again and leaves me wordless.

When the time came to leave this inner sanctum, we moved into the empty chamber to the left of Ptah's ravaged statue to collect ourselves before exiting into the bright light of morning. One of my traveling companions, Bill, had seemed particularly attuned to my inner thoughts and feelings throughout the trip. He felt certain we'd known each other before, and several times I'd had the disconcerting feeling that he somehow knew the secrets of my past lives more clearly than I did. All through our journey he seemed to be waiting for me to remember something.

As we stood recovering from the power of our collective communion with Sekhmet, Bill gave me a big hug. With a shaky voice, I said, "And the light fills every dark space." It was the best I could do to summarize all that I was feeling.

Bill hugged me tighter and whispered into my ear, "You are loved beyond measure. You *are* love. Beyond measure."

And, in that moment, I understood (or remembered) at the depth of my being the truth that had been trying to make itself known to me ever since Cameron had died, the truth that had been plain to see all along but had somehow been too simple or too obvious for me to grasp: *love is all that matters; love is the source of my being; love is the only power; love is who I am.* It was love that could now flow through all the broken places in my heart, making it not a weak and shattered thing but a wellspring of light and beauty and power.

As we stepped out of the darkened chambers of the Temple of Ptah, beams of morning light were streaming through the hypostyle hall, a seemingly endless chamber of ornately carved columns connected overhead by massive stone beams, the likes of which few modern-day cranes could lift to those heights. The rays of light streaming through these columns from strategically placed slotted windows were like the rays you sometimes see breaking through a cumulus cloud at sunset. It was the kind of light that I've always thought of as God's light. I could see individual dust motes dancing in those beams of light and my breath caught at their beauty.

In my mind, a memory arose of endless childhood hours spent with my wooden building blocks, recreating just such a space:

rows of round yellow columns topped by green rectangular lintels. I'd called them churches, but they were unlike any church I'd ever seen in *this* lifetime. Perhaps I'd remembered a life here before or dreamed ahead to this healing moment. The child that I was, the child that I still carried within me, had been trying to help me create or remember this moment of healing grace my entire life long.

As we left Karnak, we stopped at the statue of the great scarab, Kheperi: the one who births new life from shit, the one who raises the sun into the sky, the one who brings the blessing of completion. I watched as several tourists circled the god, hoping to be blessed and transformed by its powers. I knew that I'd already closed my own circle, completed one loop of the endless spiral of my own evolution, as I stood in the paradox of Sekhmet's power: the play of the dark and the light.

What I will carry with me from Karnak, forever, is the quality of light, the gentle strength and grace of Sekhmet's love, and the way they both filtered indelibly into the very fiber of my being.

The Mythology of Hathor and Sekhmet

The Egyptian pantheon of gods and goddesses can be confusing, but there is a school of interpretation which explains that the ancient Egyptians had a very clear sense of the One God. The multitude of gods and goddesses were actually "neters," or aspects of the One God.[69] This makes it easier to understand the interchangeability of gods and goddesses we sometimes see in Egyptian mythology. Every god and goddess is simply the One God expressing in a particular form. As we are all creations of God, we can also see these aspects or manifestations of God's nature within ourselves.

One Egyptian myth in particular captured my attention, for it played up the aspects of Hathor and Sekhmet as alter egos of the same being. It is the myth of the destruction of mankind.

> There came a time when the sun god Ra became impatient with the peoples of the earth. He called upon Hathor to kill everyone. Normally, Hathor was more into joyful partying, but obediently she began to do as Ra wished. In the process she became so caught up in the killing that she morphed into Sekhmet, the goddess of war and pestilence, and went a bit crazy, developing an insatiable taste for human blood. After a time, Ra repented. He decided he didn't want all of humanity destroyed. He tried to call Sekhmet off, but by this time she was deep in the throes of her bloodlust. So Ra decided to play a trick. He had thousands of gallons of beer mixed with red ochre until it made a convincing decoy for human blood. He had the fields flooded with this substance. Sekhmet arrived and, thinking she'd come upon a sea of human blood, she

> *gorged herself on the red beer. As she fell into a drunken stupor and slept, she morphed back into Hathor, the gentle goddess of joy and love. Humankind was saved from total annihilation. But Ra, overcome by the destruction he'd wrought, abdicated his throne to Thoth, the god of wisdom and the god of the scribes.[70]*

Although viewing Hathor and Sekhmet, the two goddesses to whom I felt most drawn, as alter egos held a certain mystique and appeal, the first time I heard this story it made little sense to me. As I'd discovered earlier in contemplating the face of Hathor, I simply needed time for rumination before I could find the personal meaning in this story.

When I look at the myth now, I can see how my own angry Sekhmet was the one addicted to drama and suffering. She was the one who, in the dream of the yellow car, felt the need to strike out. In the light of day, under the power of the sun god Ra, suffering and weakness were the only stories I could see. To preserve my own power, I had to disempower those around me. I took delight and reveled in the story of that drama until an almost inconceivable sacrifice was made. It took great loss before, drunk in my sorrow, figuratively and literally, I could find my way back to Hathor, my peaceful core.

It was the same struggle that I'd recognized in my earlier drawing and collage work: the battle between the dark, fearful, angry self and the light, optimistic, Pollyanna self. It took a shattering loss to set me out on a path where I could begin to recognize these two aspects of myself. But they had always been there, pulling against each other. The great mystery is that, in some way, they *are* each other.

I can begin to understand now what is meant by embracing the shadow, for we cannot disown our darker natures without also extinguishing our light. It was in reaching out to touch the heart of the dark goddess that I finally found my own light. It is not a battle where one side wins and the other is banished, but an inner alchemy of sorts. The birth, or rebirth, of the light from the dark.

The Mythology of Hathor and Sekhmet

Just as Sekhmet, the violent and vengeful goddess of war, expressed her more peaceful aspect in Hathor, the goddess of love, the gods Ra and Thoth could also be seen as alter egos. Where Ra was the god of the sun, Thoth was the god of the moon. When I was finally ready to remember the peaceful Hathor aspect of myself, Ra, the god who rules the light of day, gave way to Thoth, the god of the night, and it was my dreams that started to bring me back to my truth. Furthermore, as the god of scribes, Thoth brought the gift of literacy—record keeping and storytelling through the written word—to humankind. In my own life, this written record keeping and storytelling would be the key to resolving my grief and making sense of my experiences. It was the writing, reading and rereading of my journals that finally allowed the meaning of my story to reveal itself to me.

The meanings of the three tarot cards that had foretold the gifts of my Egyptian sojourn seemed to converge in that single magical and paradoxical encounter with Sekhmet, when the beast of the darkness became the mother who could birth the light. By discovering that beneath her ferocious exterior beat a gentle and tender heart, I was empowered to find my own strength and to recognize that it could only come from love.

Do-Overs

Not long after I returned from Egypt, I dreamed again of Cameron.

> ### *December 12, 2006 — Miracles*
>
>
>
> *I'm with Cameron and I'm marveling at how wonderful the past year has been, how good he's been–a good student, no drugs, working hard, such a nice young man. Someone thought he was on drugs because his eyes looked strange, but they tested him and he was clean. I told him his eyes had always looked like that–those beautiful, intense brown eyes. I just love him so much and I'm so grateful that at last he's turned his life around. I think what a shame it is that this will be his last year here, that he's going to die. Then something in me wells up with hope–they could be wrong, doctors can be wrong. Miracles can happen–one already has. Why not one more?*

I woke from this dream in the middle of the night so full of love and joy, thinking, "*How wonderful, how wonderful—he's a good young man, I'm proud of him, he's my joy.*" I fell back into sleep telling him over and over again how much I loved him, my beautiful boy. In the morning I awoke with the chorus of a Christmas carol singing through my mind:

> Ah, ah, beautiful is the Mother.
> Ah, ah, beautiful is her Son.[71]

It seemed to me that wherever he was now, everything was all right. All those things I'd seen as broken in him, and in me, were healed. I wasn't sure what to make of the idea that he'd be gone in a year. I suspected it might mean he would be ready to move on and reincarnate. Part of me felt a little reluctant for that and I wondered if my connection to him would be lost at that point. There were so many mysteries about how it all worked and I couldn't quite sort it out in my mind. Still, the dream had felt so full of love and joy that I knew somehow we had created a miracle together. We were both whole again.

A few months later, a series of dreams of Cameron as a baby and then a young child began. In the first of these, Cameron is a baby and I pick him up. I'm surprised at how heavy he is. I fall over backward and the baby cries and cries.

In another dream, Cameron is a toddler, maybe three years old. I lift him into bed with us and he's so heavy. It feels very real, as though the weight and warmth of his body is actually filling the space in the bed between David and me.

Then came this dream:

February 16, 2007 — Don't Take My Toys

I am loading things in boxes for a yard sale or to give them to charity or throw them out. Cameron goes through a box that has some of his old toys in it. He doesn't want me to get rid of those. He is a young boy of five or six.

In the hypnagogic it was crystal clear to me that Cameron was not done playing with his toys. It was like his toys had been taken from him forcefully and not freely given. At first I thought Cameron might be protesting his death, but then I remembered that he often complained as a young man that he'd never really gotten to be a child, to have a childhood. I think even while he was alive he felt robbed. It seemed like he might be visiting me now as a child in order to reclaim the childhood he thought he'd missed.

The journey of grief is such a crazy roller-coaster ride. Just when you think you've really turned the corner and stripped away the last remnants of remorse and sadness, another layer surfaces to be examined. It's like a huge onion that you just keep peeling away, one tearful layer at a time. This last dream revealed yet another layer of guilt in me. Even though I knew Cameron was okay now and that all was well between us, I still felt bad about the pain he'd endured in his childhood as his ADHD and our expectations so often collided in battle.

As fate would have it, I'd made plans to return to the El Rocio Retreat Center to watch the CJEA student I was mentoring deliver her supervised workshop. I would stay for most of the intensive and have ample opportunity to explore this next layer of the onion as we collaged and journaled our way through the week.

During the intensive, we did a journaling exercise in which we let our critical voice speak and then answered back to it. My critical voice was brutal. After a hurling at me a string of complaints about my wasting time, getting nowhere and accomplishing nothing, the critic brought out the big guns.

"Hey, good for you," the voice lashed out. *"Your kid's dead now and so you can just go and have the time of your life. Hooray for you. Dumb Shit."*

I was stunned. No one can be as cruel as one's own inner voice, for it is privy to one's weakest points and deepest fears. Here was the crux of my guilt: I was free to live my life any way I wanted and Cameron wasn't. Oh, yes, I knew he was still living in some form, I knew he was still learning, growing and experiencing. But the idea that my freedom in this life had been gained at his expense still rankled.

Yet as my turn came to talk back to the critic, I realized something. *"Stop it! Stop it!"* I wrote. *"It's **your** fucking voice that hurt Cameron so bad. All you know how to do is hurt people. You are dead wrong about all of it. You have no right to hurt me like this. Get out of my head!"*

In the voice of the inner critic, I had recognized the violent beast, the bloodthirsty side of Sekhmet. However Egypt had shown me that the beast could be tamed, that underneath it all the only true power was love. Every moment of my life would provide a new opportunity to choose which power would fuel me: fear or love.

On our free day, I drove once again to South Padre Island. As I walked on the beach there, thoughts and words were flooding through my mind, so I sat down to do some journaling.

March 28, 2007, South Padre Island

I'm walking and I'm looking for that special shell or stone—that magical reminder of your love, Cameron. I wonder what stage I'm at now in this dance? Was it only last year that I found the stone with the heart carved into it the moment I stepped onto the beach? Time has no frame of reference for me on this path, except when it is punctuated by birthdays or anniversaries. In a few days, you would have been 29. I've been dreaming of you as a child. How old are you where you are? Oh, my lovely little boy, I still carry so much sorrow for what I've done to you.

As I walk looking for a message from you, I realize that I am looking to you for comfort—still expecting you to be the grownup, expecting you to be my source of wisdom and hope. How unfair and needy I can be. My lovely little boy, I am so sorry no one ever told you how special and amazing you were. What a gift and a treasure. I see now how my viciously critical voice could turn on you so quickly and unfairly. I see how you were made to hold the shadow selves for all of us—the ones we would not admit to in ourselves. You were our scapegoat. I feel so sad sometimes for the immense un-redoableness of it all. There are no do-overs, are there? Not here anyway. God, can this still be healed even now? I have to pray, believing, that it can and it will.

> *Cameron, I'm always wanting you to give me a shell or a stone, but what do I have to give you? I don't know how this all works. Can you walk on a beach somewhere where you are and can my love create a message for you there? Something you can pick up and hold close to your heart?*

Menita had said that when feelings of sadness and guilt arose, I should acknowledge them, but not give them life by naming them or attaching them to any event. He told me that when they arose, I should say, "I love you, that's all," and let it go. I put my journal back in my beach bag then and I drew a giant heart in the sand. I wrote in it: "Cameron, I'm sorry. I love you!" Then I stepped into the ocean and let the surf wash over me and fill me with that sense of eternity and spiritual connection that only the sea can bring.

I don't know how long I stayed there in the water, but when I got out, the tide had come up and swept my message out into the rolling surf and, I hoped, delivered it to my son. Perhaps, somewhere in that other realm, Cameron was walking on a beach and my love washed up on the shore at his feet in the form of a heart-shaped shell. I hoped it was a great big one.

A few nights later, a dream came in answer to my question about do-overs.

> ### March 31, 2007 — Do-Overs
>
>
>
> *Cameron is a little boy of about 6. He is sad and crying. At first I don't understand why he's so sad and I grow a bit impatient. But then I realize he's just feeling the unfairness and injustice of things. He lays across my lap with his back up and I just rub his back and soothe him.*
>
> *Next he's standing by a door, as if he's about to walk through it. I rub his hair and head and something just washes over me. I realize there's some kind of time warp going on here and I <u>can</u> go back and heal the little child of the past. I can love Cameron the way I should have. I have twenty-some years to do it right this time before it's time for him to go.*

The dream seemed to confirm that through the magic of collapsible time and intersecting dimensions, all the wounds of the past could be healed in the present. It was not too late. It would never be too late. Do-overs *were* possible and they were happening right now—in my heart and in my dreams.

It occurred to me that Cameron's position, lying across my knees, was the traditional position for delivering a spanking. He had experienced more than his share of spankings as a child, but in the dream I transformed that position into one of healing and love instead of pain, anger and judgment.

That simple motion of my hand gently stroking my little boy's back was an act of redemption and atonement. Somehow, it left Cameron free to walk through that doorway and into his future carrying nothing but love.

Epilogue: New Beginnings

*E*very ending holds its own beginning and every beginning knows its end, my dream lizards once told me. Yet, in the journey of life we are always somewhere between the two, somewhere within the looping spirals of our own evolution. While this book has reached an end, my journey (and yours) continues. New beginnings are made, new endings are reached and the circle keeps reaching for its next conclusion and its next birth.

It's clear to me now that what's left of Cameron is so much more than just those smelly socks. What's left of him is what was always the truth of him: wholeness and love. His death helped me to unravel my own story and to imagine it in a better light. I am forever grateful that his passing helped me to discover (or remember) the deeper truths of my own existence and the eternal and infinite power of love. What a gift.

This past December, I celebrated my 50th birthday on the island of Kauai with my family around me: David, Ryan, Sarah and her husband Justin, and the first member of our next generation, my grandson, Mace Alexander. I'm certain Cameron was with us, too.

December 16, 2007, Kekaha, Kauai

An early morning walk on the lovely beach in front of our rental house. The sunrise was beautiful. The sea was breaking in big, glorious waves, and my feet were sinking luxuriously into the soft sugar sand with every step. I found a lovely spot under a small pine tree where I could sit comfortably on the ledge of sand created by the highest tide. I closed my eyes and took a few deep breaths and just listened to the sound of the surf, allowing myself to be filled with peace.

When I opened my eyes they were drawn to a small seedpod in the sand that looked to me like a

Epilogue: New Beginnings

perfect little heart. I acknowledged Cameron's presence and wished him a good morning.

I thought to myself how nice it was to be able to think of him with love and pleasure and realized that, in an odd way, his death had allowed me to stop worrying about him. Now that he's dead, I no longer have *to worry about him—and in a way that means I never really* did *have to worry about him, since his potential death was the overarching worry I always held. Too bad I didn't realize that while he was alive.*

But I feel the difference in all my other relationships—worry is so senseless. I want my children and grandchildren to live their lives and be happy and take risks and make mistakes and just LIVE. As the younger generation says, "It's all good."

As I rose to walk back to the house, I picked up the little pod and found it to be interestingly bumpy and lovely, but not really heart-shaped at all. Rather round and ordinary with a slightly pointy bottom. What occurred to me then was that from a certain angle, with a special quality of light, it could look quite like a heart.

And isn't that true about how we look at things in general? Every common, ordinary moment— every common, ordinary event, unexamined, may look quite plain. But with a minor adjustment of perspective and a certain quality of inner light, suddenly every situation can be seen with love and AS love. Every one.

As I began the walk back, I found a piece of coral that the tide had washed in. I hadn't noticed any coral on the walk up—I'd actually been surprised not to see a single shell or anything. I picked up the piece of coral and suddenly saw a few more pieces, then a few more. I flashed back to that moment in Rocky Point when I'd looked down and seen a million little heart-shaped shell fragments all around my feet.

It seemed to me that somehow, once you start seeing something—like heart-shaped shells or washed up coral, somehow your eye becomes attuned or entrained to that shape or that object and you begin to see it everywhere. Couldn't one's heart and spirit just as easily become attuned? Attuned to love and to peace, rather than to worry and pain?

So, if it's just simple attunement or perspective, then is that an illusion? Or a delusion? Or is it a reality that you've just been blind to—blinded by fear, worry or just plain disinterest? If it is an illusion, still I'll take it. Isn't it nicer to live with a feeling of love and peace than constant fear and worry? And don't we create our reality by how we see things and feel things?

I choose to remain content with my own certain perspective and a particular quality of light that allows me to enjoy the peace of seeing love everywhere.

Author's Note

Often, another's healing or spiritual journey is too personal to speak to others. The experiences of that person and the steps they took on their journey may feel far removed from your own experience.

Still, I hope that something in my journey spoke to you and that you will want to examine how it might apply to your own life. Indeed, knowing the way the Universe works, I can't imagine that you are here, reading these words, unless you were meant to be.

If you are grieving, then I hope you will explore some of the tools I used to journey through my own process of grief: journaling, art, the practice of dreaming, and the guidance of synchronicity. I hope you will recognize that, as painful as your loss truly is, there is a gift wrapped within it. That gift is the call to the re-membrance and re-creation of yourself.

Know, too, that grief takes many forms. It may not be that you lost a child or a spouse or someone very close to you. It may be that you lost a job, or a home, or a way of life with which you identified. It may be that you are struggling with a health challenge. It may be that you see a situation in the world around you—poverty, war, injustice, pain—that breaks your heart. If so, know that the loss of identity and the breaking of your heart is an invitation to greater wholeness. It is the broken places that will allow the light to shine through.

Please recognize that grief is not the only impetus for this journey. Anyone can undertake the journey back to the truth of the inner self at any time. This was my journey long before grief arrived to speed the process along.

Whether yours is a journey of grief or simply a journey of self-discovery, you can explore additional resources for personal growth and awakening at *www.DeepWaterLeafSociety.com*. Whatever brought you to be holding this book in your hands, remember it is no accident. Your own Big Story is chasing you.

The Deep Water Leaf Society

And so, I invite you to join the *Deep Water Leaf Society*, a borderless club that welcomes anyone who is willing to look deeper and to see that we are all so much more than our drama, so much more than our karma, so much more than the smelly socks we may leave behind.

Every story is sacred. Every person is whole. And love is the only power behind it all.

Notes

---

[1] See groups.yahoo.com/group/griefsteps_gensupport on the Internet.

[2] "Time." Words and Music by Roger Waters. Performed by Pink Floyd on the album *Dark Side of the Moon*.

[3] For more information about Dr. Capacchione and the CJEA program, visit www.luciac.com.

[4] Lucia Capacchione, Ph.D., A.T.R. *Visioning:Ten Steps to Designing the Life of Your Dreams* (New York: Tarcher/Putnam, 2000).

[5] Visioning® is the method originated by Dr. Lucia Capacchione, and described in her book, *Visioning: Ten Steps to Designing the Life of Your Dreams* (Tarcher/Putnam).

[6] Jill Neimark. "God, Physics and Turtle Soup." (Interview with Paul Davies and Margaret Wertheim.) *Science & Spirit*, July/Aug 2002.

[7] "Be Yourself." "Daily Guide" for May 30. *Science of Mind*, May 2003.

[8] For more information about Padre Pio, you may wish to review the following books and websites:
Fransican Friars of the Immaculate. *Padre Pio: The Wonder Worker* (Waite Park, Minnesota: Park Press, 1999).
Renzo Allegri. *Padre Pio: Man of Hope* (Cincinnati: Servant Books, 2000).
"Pio of Pietrelcina" in *Wikipedia,* http://en.wikipedia.org/wiki/Padre_Pio.
Padre Pio Foundation, http://www.padrepio.com.

[9] This story can be found in many books and websites. See, for example:
Renzo Allegri. *Padre Pio: Man of Hope* (Cincinnati: Servant Books, 2000), 169.
"A Blind Girl." http://successprayer.com/placesofmiracle.html.
http://www.catholicwebservices.com/ENGLISH/Healings.htm.

[10] Lucia Capacchione, Ph.D. *Recovery of Your Inner Child* (New York: Simon & Schuster, 1991).

[11] Lucia Capacchione, Ph.D. *The Creative Journal: The Art of Finding Yourself*, 2nd ed. (Franklin Lakes: Career Press, 2002), 119-23.

[12] Ibid., 22-7.

[13] Robert Moss. *Conscious Dreaming* (New York: Three Rivers Press, 1996), 199.

[14] Lucia Capacchione, Ph.D. *Recovery of Your Inner Child* (New York: Simon & Schuster, 1991), 190-200.

[15] Claire Perkins. "Drowning." First appeared in *Maricopa Community Colleges: Creative Writing Competition 1995 – 1996 Anthology*, 3.

[16] Robert Moss. *Conscious Dreaming* (New York: Three Rivers Press, 1996), 64-5, 152-3.

[17] Robert Moss. *The Three "Only" Things: Tapping the Power of Dreams, Coincidence & Imagination* (Novato, California: New World Library, 2007), 192-9.

[18] "Bridge Over Troubled Water." Words and Music by Paul Simon. Performed by Simon and Garfunkel on the album *Bridge Over Troubled Water* (Columbia Records, 1969).

[19] "Oh, Very Young." Words and Music by Cat Stevens. From the album *Buddha in the Chocolate Box* (Island Records, 1974). Used by permission.

[20] "Building a Mystery." Words and Music by Sarah McLachlan and Pierre Marchand. Performed and recorded live by Sarah McLachlan on the album *Mirrorball* (Arista, 1999).

[21] "Hold On." Words and Music by Sarah McLachlan. Performed and recorded live by Sarah McLachlan on the album *Mirrorball* (Arista, 1999).

[22] "Angel." Words and Music by Sarah McLachlan. Performed and recorded live by Sarah McLachlan on the album *Mirrorball* (Arista, 1999).

[23] "Dante's Prayer." Words and Music by Loreena McKennitt. Performed by Loreena McKennitt on the album *The Book of Secrets* (Quinlan Road Ltd., 1997).

[24] "Love Is." Words and Music by John Keller, Tonio K. and Michael Caruso. Performed by Vanessa Williams and Brian McKnight on the album *Beverly Hills 90210 Soundtrack* (Giant Records, 1992).

[25] "As." Words and Music by Stevie Wonder. Copyright 1975 (renewed 2003) JOBETE MUSIC CO., INC. and BLACK BULL MUSIC, c/o EMI APRIL MUSIC INC. All rights reserved; international copyright secured. Used by permission.

[26] "A New Day Has Come." Words and Music Aldo Novo and Stephan Moccio. Performed by Celine Dion on the album *A New Day Has Come* (Epic, 2002).

[27] Robert Moss. *The Dreamer's Book of the Dead: A Soul Traveler's Guide to Death, Dying and the Other Side* (Rochester, Vermont: Destiny Books, 2005). See especially 54-76.

[28] This is the journaling dialogue method as it was taught during the CJEA training. See also: Lucia Capacchione, Ph.D., A.T.R. *Visioning:Ten Steps to Designing the Life of Your Dreams* (New York: Tarcher/Putnam, 2000), 129-45.

[29] Robert Moss. *The Three "Only" Things: Tapping the Power of Dreams, Coincidence & Imagination* (Novato, California: New World Library, 2007), 1-4.

[30] "I Will Remember You." Words and Music by Sarah McLachlan, Seamus Egan and Dave Merenda. Performed by Sarah McLachlan on the album *Mirrorball* (Arista,1999).

[31] For information on the El Rocio Retreat Center, visit www.elrocioretreat.com.

[32] Lucia Capacchione, Ph.D. *Recovery of Your Inner Child* (New York: Simon & Schuster, 1991). For an overview of the Inner Child, see 16-25, 47-54. For an overview of the Nurturing Parent see 117-20. For an overview of the Protective Parent see 145-54. For an overview of the Critical Parent see 167-71.

[33] James Van Praagh. *Healing Grief: Reclaiming Life After any Loss* (New York: Dutton, 2000). For more information on the psychic medium James Van Praagh, see www.vanpraagh.com.

[34] For information on the psychic medium John Edward, see www.johnedward.net.

[35] "The Reason." Words and Music by Daniel Estrin and Douglas Robb, Copyright 2003, WB MUSIC CORP. and SPREAD YOUR CHEEKS AND PUSH OUT THE MUSIC. All rights Administered by WB MUSIC CORP. All Rights Reserrved. Used by permission of ALFRED PUBLISHING CO., INC.

[36] See groups.yahoo.com/group/griefsteps_gensupport on the Internet. This community was started by Brook Noel, co-author with Pamela D. Blair Ph.D. of *I Wasn't Ready to Say Goodbye: Surviving, Coping & Healing after the Sudden Death of a Loved One* (Milwaukee: Champion Press, 2000).

[37] Don Miguel Ruiz. *The Four Agreements: A Practical Guide to Personal Freedom* (San Rafael, California, 1997), 109-13.

[38] For more information on the psychic medium Allison DuBois, see www.allisondubois.com.

[39] For information on the Southwest Institute of Healing Arts, see www.swiha.edu.

[40] For information on the Arizona Holistic Chamber of Commerce, see www.azholisticchamber.com.

[41] For information about the psychic medium Jamie Clark, see www.jamieclark.net.

[42] "Ain't No Mountain High Enough." Words and Music by Nikolas Ashford and Valerie Simpson. Copyright 1967, 1970 (renewed 1995, 1998) JOBETE MUCIS CO., INC. All rights controlled and administered by EMI APRIL MUSIC INC. All rights reserved and international copyright secured. Used by permission.

[43] "Heart of the Matter." Words and Music by Don Henley, Mike Campbell and J. D. Souther. Performed by India.Arie on the album *Testimony: Vol 1, Life & Relationship* (Motown, 2006).

[44] "Love's Divine." Words and Music by Mark Batson and Seal Samuel. Performed by Seal on the album *Seal IV* (Warner Bros. Records, 2003).

[45] "String of Pearls." By Michael Franks. Copyright 1993, Mississippi Mud Music Co. Reprinted with permission of the author. From the album *Dragonfly Summer* (Reprise Records, 1993).

[46] Dan Millman. *The Life You Were Born to Live: A Guide to Finding Your Life Purpose* (Tiburon, California: H J Kramer Inc, 1993), 202-5.

[47] For more information about Dr. Neddermeyer, visit www.gen-assist.com.

[48] Nell Minow. "Learning to Forgive." www.beliefnet.com/story/183/story_18353_1.html. Rcd. via email January 2006.

[49] "Love's Divine." Words and Music by Mark Batson and Seal Samuel. Performed by Seal on the album *Seal IV* (Warner Bros. Records, 2003).

[50] C. S. Lewis. *The Horse and His Boy* (C. S. Lewis Pte. Ltd., 1954) as it appears in the collection *The Chronicles of Narnia* (New York: Harper/Collins), 199-309. The story of Aravis is summarized from several chapters of the book and the direct quote (Aslan speaking) is on page 299.

[51] Philip Pullman. *His Dark Materials*. This trilogy includes *The Golden Compass* (1995), *The Subtle Knife* (1997), *The Amber Spyglass* (2000) as collected in the boxed set (New York: Alfred A. Knopf, revised Knopf trade paperback edition 2002). The theme of Lyra having a great destiny which she must not be told is woven throughout the stories.

[52] What I refer to as "cellular release" is a shorthand description for the energy methods Sherry Anshara teaches in her "Intuitive Powers/Practical Applications I" workshop. For more information see www.quantumpathic.com.

[53] For more information on John and Carmen LaMarca and the WholeLife Pages directory, see www.wholelifepages.com.

[54] For more information about Sheila Reed and Luminati Egyptian Travel, see www.luminati.net.

[55] For more information about the Arizona Holistic Chamber of Commerce's Internet radio program, *A New Spirit of Business*, or to listen to archived recordings of the program, see www.achieveradio.com/holistic.

[56] For more information about Achieve Radio or to listen to live or archived Internet radio broadcasts, see www.achieveradio.com.

[57] For more information about Sherri Devereau or her book, *Shadows on my Shift: Real Life Stories of a Psychic EMT* (New River Press, 2006), see www.intuitiveeyes.com or www.shadowsonmyshift.net.

[58] Cherie Bennett and Jeff Gottesfeld. *Broken Bridges*. Movie. Directed by Steven Goldmann. Produced by Chickflicks Productions/CMT Films/MTV Films/Paramount Home Entertainment. Distributed by Paramount Classics, 2006.

[59] "Broken." Words and Music by Angela Peters Lauer, Hillary Lee Lindsey and Angelo T. Petraglia. Performed by Lindsey Haun on the album *Broken Bridges: Original Motion Picture Soundtrack* (Show Dog Records, 2006).

[60] Normandi Ellis. *Dreams of Isis: A Woman's Spiritual Sojourn* (Wheaton, Illinois; Quest Books, 1995), 44.

[61] Rose-Marie Hagen and Rainer Hagen. *Egypt: People, Gods, Pharaohs* (Los Angeles; Taschen, 2002), 176. See also Lorna Oakes and Lucia Gahlin. *Ancient Egypt: An Illustrated Reference to the Myths, Religions, Pyramids and Temples of the Land of the Pharaohs* (New York: Barnes & Noble Publishing, 2006), 156, 227, 287, 328-9, 409. See also Normandi Ellis. *Dreams of Isis: A Woman's Spiritual Sojourn* (Wheaton, Illinois: Quest Books, 1995), 37.

[62] Normandi Ellis. *Dreams of Isis: A Woman's Spiritual Sojourn* (Wheaton, Illinois: Quest Books, 1995), 40-1.

[63] Ibid., 160-1.

[64] Ibid., 161.

[65] As related by our Egyptologist, Soheila, during the course of our journey. See also Lorna Oakes and Lucia Gahlin. *Ancient Egypt: An Illustrated Reference to the Myths, Religions, Pyramids and Temples of the Land of the Pharaohs* (New York: Barnes & Noble Publishing, 2006), 308-9. See also Normandi Ellis. *Dreams of Isis: A Woman's Spiritual Sojourn* (Wheaton, Illinois, 1995), 275-8.

[66] As related by our Egyptologist, Soheila, during the course of our journey. See also Rose-Marie Hagen and Rainer Hagen. *Egypt: People, Gods, Pharaohs* (Los Angeles: Taschen, 2002), 180. See also Lorna Oakes and Lucia Gahlin. *Ancient Egypt: An Illustrated Reference to the Myths, Religions, Pyramids and Temples of the Land of the Pharaohs* (New York: Barnes & Noble Publishing, 2006), 167, 175.

[67] Lorna Oakes and Lucia Gahlin. *Ancient Egypt: An Illustrated Reference to the Myths, Religions, Pyramids and Temples of the Land of the Pharaohs* (New York: Barnes & Noble Publishing, 2006), 167-9, 182-3.

[68] Ibid. 173.

[69] Moustafa Gadalla. *Egypt: A Practical Guide* (Greensboro, North Carolina:Tehuti Research Foundation, 1998), 64-7.

[70] The myth of the destruction of mankind is retold here in my own words and interpretation based on the story as told by our Egyptologist, Soheila, and as related in Lorna Oakes and Lucia Gahlin. *Ancient Egypt: An Illustrated Reference to the Myths, Religions, Pyramids and Temples of the Land of the Pharaohs* (New York: Barnes & Noble Publishing, 2006), 168, 320-1.

[71] "Bring a Torch, Jeanette, Isabella." A 16th Century Christmas carol, which originated in the Provence region of France, first published in 1553. English translation dates to the 18th Century.

www.ingramcontent.com/pod-product-compliance
Lightning Source LLC
Chambersburg PA
CBHW051423290426
44109CB00016B/1406